▲ *The Place of A Thousand Drips*

Waterfalls & Cascades
Of The Great Smoky Mountains

Hal Hubbs, Charles Maynard & David Morris

Panther Press SEYMOUR TENNESSEE

This book is for Elizabeth, Janice and Lin who share our lives and our love of the mountains.

The Trails Illustrated Topo Map of the Great Smoky Mountains National Park and the Great Smoky Mountains National Park Recreation Map by Trails Illustrated are some of the most accurate maps of the Great Smoky Mountains National Park and mark the falls that are listed in this book. They can be ordered from: Trails Illustrated, P.O. Box 3610, Evergreen, Colorado 80439
1-800-962-1643

Published by Panther Press
213 Ledwell Drive
Seymour, Tennessee 37865

International Standard Book Number 0-9630682-4-5
Printed in the United States of America.

Cover photograph by Hal Hubbs
Back cover photographs by Hal Hubbs and David Morris
Photo credits: Hal Hubbs pgs. 27, 33, 36, 37, 44, 45, 49, 52, 53, 57, 60, 61, 64, 68 & 71. David Morris pgs. 33, 40, 41, 48, 52 & 56. National Park Service pgs. 2, 9, 19 & 30.
Maps by Charles Maynard
Cover & book design by Robyn Rusk Graphic Design
702 Comer Circle, Dandridge, Tennessee 37725

Acknowledgments: *We are grateful for the assistance of many who helped us prepare this book. Our children, Brian, Caroline, Anna, Ben and John helped us to measure and photograph many falls. Glenn Cardwell, Supervisory Park Ranger at Sugarlands, Annette Evans, Park Librarian, Kitty Manscill, Museum Curator, Gene Cox, Chief of Visitor Services, Eldon Wanrow, Supervisory Park Ranger at Cades Cove and Donna Lane, NHA Sales Coordinator at Sugarlands were all most helpful with information and suggestions. Elizabeth Hubbs, Lin Morris, Janice Maynard and Nancy Best proofread and edited.*

Waterfalls and cascades are beautiful but potentially dangerous. Please use every precaution and good sense when visiting the park and its falls. Observe all posted warnings. The authors and publisher are not responsible for injury, loss or damage incurred from the use of this guide.

Table of Contents

▲ *Rainbow Falls*

▲ *Ramsay Cascade*

Introduction

Waterfalls and cascades cannot be adequately captured in words or photographs. They must be seen, experienced. This book attempts to point out interesting features and the location of over thirty falls and cascades in the Great Smoky Mountains National Park. Not all of the falls in the park are included. This book calls attention to some of the more spectacular or accessible falls and cascades of the Smokies.

For purposes of clarity, the terms "waterfall" and "cascade" designate two types of phenomena. "Waterfall" is water in a vertical or free fall over a cliff. Only a few falls actually free fall away from a rocky face. Rainbow and Grotto Falls are two of the primary examples. "Cascade" is used to describe water as it rushes down rocks and rocky ledges. Ramsay Cascade and Laurel Falls are good examples of this. However, the lines are blurred in many instances. Gunter Fork and Juneywhank Falls can fit both categories. It's a challenge to describe the elusive, liquid nature of falls and cascades.

Measuring the falls presents another challenge. Where does a cascade begin or end? Is a steep cascade above or below a falls included? Is a cascade measured by its fall in elevation or by the distance it travels? All these questions and more present themselves to observers of creeks and streams of the park.

For cascades, both the fall or drop in elevation as well as the distance the water travels over the rocks are provided. Gunter Fork falls 100 feet and travels 285 feet. Huskey Branch travels 120 feet but only falls about 50 feet. For free falling water, the distance the water falls from cliff top to rocky base or plunge pool is measured.

Measurements were made with a plumb line and altimeter to give the best guesses on the height and distance of the falls. The descriptions of the falls include directional notes (right and left). The orientation is always as if the observer is facing the falls.

When planning to see a waterfall, bear in mind that rainfall has a direct effect on how much water will be in the stream. The rainfall chart below shows that September and October are the driest months while July is among one of the wettest. It is disappointing to find only a trickle when a falls is expected. The precipitation is greater for the higher elevations. Waterflow is dependent on the total area drained by the creek as well as rainfall. The waterflow chart below indicates some streams and their volume of water.

As beautiful as waterfalls and cascades are they can be most dangerous. Stay on established and maintained trails. These have been constructed for your safety. Observe all warning signs. Use common sense. Wet, moss-covered rocks are slippery. Ice coats the rocks beside streams and falls in the winter. In the summer it's fun to splash and play in the cool mountain streams. In the winter it can be deadly.

The terrain of the park and its annual rainfall of over 85 inches make for an abundance of falls and cascades. Enjoy this beautiful and magical feature of the Great Smoky Mountains National Park.

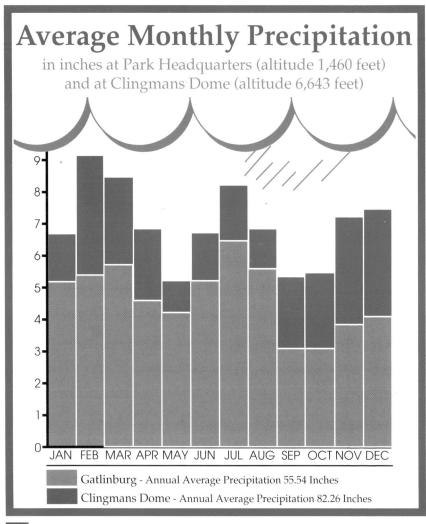

Average Monthly Precipitation

in inches at Park Headquarters (altitude 1,460 feet) and at Clingmans Dome (altitude 6,643 feet)

Gatlinburg - Annual Average Precipitation 55.54 Inches

Clingmans Dome - Annual Average Precipitation 82.26 Inches

Streamflow Chart

Streamflow is determined by many factors including the square miles drained by the stream, the altitude of the headwaters and the rainfall. This chart is based on average flow which is figured in cubic feet of water per second.

LeConte Creek	11.23
Chasteen Creek	14
Roaring Fork	17.64
Indian Creek	23.97
Lynn Camp Prong	45.6
Big Creek	56.1
Twentymile Creek	58.89
Deep Creek	133.3
Hazel Creek	150.6

Timeless Waters

Beside Grotto Falls only the sound of Roaring Fork can be heard. The water falling off the overhanging ledge of sandstone fills the air with mist. All other sounds of the forest are blocked out. Even conversation becomes impossible. A friend and I yelled at each other simply to be heard. No birds, no rush of wind through the leaves, no hammering of woodpeckers, nor swish of leaves underfoot. Nothing but the sound of water.

Upon listening carefully I discovered that the falls have two distinct sounds. One is a SSSHHH sound of drops leaving the cliff and falling through the air. The other sound is the splash and roar of water striking the rocks and pool below. This sound overpowers all noise. Stand at the foot of Grotto, Rainbow, Laurel, any falls. Let the sounds silence you long enough to hear the story of the mountains, a story best told at the waterfalls.

The rock walls, the jumble of smooth stones tell the story of forces that formed the mountains. Water and gravity shape the Great Smoky Mountains. When the two combine to make waterfalls and cascades, the results are fascinating and beautiful as well as formative. Due to annual precipitation equal to that of a rain forest and rugged topography, waterfalls and cascades abound along the 700 miles of streams in the Great Smoky Mountains.

The Smokies were and are carved by water. Water has shaped the mountains and valleys into their present form. Stand on a peak to look down on the jumble of mountains, ridges, valleys and ravines. Look carefully. Notice the slopes, the peaks, the twinkle of sunlight on water. Water sculpted this marvelous landscape.

At waterfalls this creative action is most dramatic. A torrent pours over cliff or bare rock face to plunge into a deep pool. Large logs against the escarpment, smooth boulders and pebbles are evidence of the power of water to move, to shape, to carve the terrain.

Water isn't the only tool that built the mountains. Over 225 million years ago the earth's crust shifted in ways that pushed up an enormous mountain range higher than today's Rockies. The rocks that were exposed as they were forced upward had been formed 375 million to 775 million years before. The original mountains were worn down by the erosive action of water until only a plain was left. More warping of the surface due to crustal movements caused the plain to rise above sea level. Water continued to cut through this plain.

Today's Smokies are actually a result of the water erosion cutting through the primal plain. The landscape has been described as one of "valleys cut between ridges rather than that of ridges rising between valleys." However, it's not the water that does the wearing, the cutting. Stone, logs, rocks, grains of sand all borne by the streams wear away the mountains. It could be said that water assists the mountains to break down themselves.

From where does this water come? The Smokies receive an average of 84 inches of precipitation each year in the highest elevations. Of that precipitation over 40% evaporates or is used by plants. Water in the air is one reason the mountains are "smoky." The mist of the mountains often obscures the terrain that is being worn away.

In addition to the land, waterfalls break down light itself. Sunlight is shattered into colored frequencies as it passes through the refracting mist of falling water. The sunlight sifting through the trees strikes Rainbow Falls, Ramsay Cascades, or Abrams Falls only to be broken into colors. Just as the strata of rock are revealed at the falls, the strata of light are seen in the rainbows and double rainbows of the falls.

Loren Eisley wrote, "If there is magic on this planet, it is contained in water." Water certainly contains some of the magic of the mountains. The streams brim with life. The thick stands of rhododendron, ferns and wildflowers crowd creek banks as evidences of the magical force. Deer, bear, snakes, otters, wolves, crayfish and salamanders are only a few of the myriad animals that drink from or live in the water that rushes down the mountains.

The Cherokee, native Americans who lived in the area before the settlers came, said the waters of the mountains were inhabited by the Nunne'hi, the water spirits. The Cherokee built villages beside the swift currents of mountain rivers. Settlers followed this example in building their own dwellings and farms. They put the fall of water to use with mills which ground grain into meal and sawed timber into lumber to sustain and shelter life.

Humans have endangered the miracle of the mountain waters over the years. Logging stripped the mountains of vegetation and took a toll in the streams. Native brook trout were choked in the silt-filled waters. Animals were unable to live in the open, logged areas. Water's force was magnified since fewer roots were unable to check its power. With the creation of the national park logging ceased and the mountains began to regenerate. Life's return to the naked chines was a magic assisted through the abundance of water.

Former inhabitants of the Smokies once returned to visit cemeteries and to drink from mountain springs. Although it's now unsafe to drink from the streams, those settlers once said, "Mountain water is healthier. It'll make yore days longer." Some drank the water's magic to live longer, remember better.

Stories are told of an earlier time when houses were built not for the view but for the availability of water. Today rotting logs and foundation stones lie beside creeks to remind of another day's dependence on the mountain's plentiful supply of water.

Waterfalls concentrate the magic of water into a sensory experience. The wetness of the mist cools hot skin. The crisp taste refreshes the weary traveler while the smell of thick vegetation speaks of life. Watching the falling water induces a trance which pushes aside all concerns. The sound, the double sound of a waterfall, overpowers until nothing else but the falls can be heard, seen, tasted, smelled, felt. Then the mountains can be experienced. Stand at Grotto, at Rainbow, at Laurel, at Abrams, at any of the hundreds of falls and cascades in the Smokies. Experience the miracle of this planet in the fall of water.   *-CWM*

Big Creek

Big Creek is one of the most scenic creeks in the entire park. From the Walnut Bottom area to its junction with the Pigeon River, Big Creek drops about 1,200 feet (120 stories), or an average of 200 feet per mile. The change in elevation causes many beautiful cascades and small falls on this large creek. The trail stays close to the creek so that its sights and sounds can be fully enjoyed. The cascades and falls that are on Big Creek and its tributaries are some of the most beautiful in the area.

The Big Creek basin was logged by the Crestmont Lumber Company in the early 1900s. Many of the trails follow old logging railroad beds. Evidence of the logging days can be found - steel cables, rails, spikes, old road beds. The forest, mostly hardwoods and spruce-fir, has recovered well from being logged.

To reach Big Creek, take the Waterville Exit on I-40 about 60 miles east of Knoxville or 50 miles west of Asheville. Cross the Pigeon River and turn left at the end of the bridge over which the Appalachian Trail crosses. Follow the road past the Waterville Power Plant to an intersection two miles from the interstate. Continue straight through the intersection up a narrow road to the Ranger Station. The picnic area and campground are beyond the ranger station about 0.8 miles. These are closed in the winter.

This area is popular due to its closeness to the interstate and its wilderness setting. The falls and cascades are without equal. A map of the area is on page 77.

Midnight Hole
•Double Falls   •8 Foot Drop

Midnight Hole is well named. A huge pool over 80 feet across and 15 feet deep is filled with the clear water of Big Creek. The pool is a dark green in winter and dark as midnight in the summer. Enormous boulders squeeze Big Creek to a small 15 foot opening through which two falls of eight feet pour. The stream on the right is the stronger of the two. In wet weather, water spills over the rock that divides the two to form a single falls. The beauty of the setting of the falls at Midnight Hole more than makes up for what the falls lack in height. For a photograph of Midnight Hole see page 52.

The fine-grained gray boulders are Thunderhead Sandstone. They provide wonderful places for picnics or spots to fish. Fishermen love the area for the easily located trout that populate the clear waters of Big Creek. An iron rail beside Midnight Hole is a reminder of the logging days at the turn of the century. Midnight Hole is an extra special place in a gorgeous valley.

To Get There: A 2.8 mile roundtrip EASY walk.

Begin on the Big Creek Trail at the Big Creek Campground beyond the ranger station. Walk up the trail 1.4 miles. Midnight Hole is on the left. Horse racks are available. The walk is on an old jeep road that is wide and gently graded so that even the inexperienced hiker can make it. With a little more time and energy it's only .6 miles to Mouse Creek Falls (see below). In the winter, remember to add 1.6 miles roundtrip distance due to the gate being closed near the ranger station.

Mouse Creek Falls
•Cascade   •50 Foot Drop

[map p. 30]

Mouse Creek Falls is a beautiful hour glass shaped cascade at the mouth of Mouse Creek. Several streams twine together to pass through a four foot opening before spreading again to form a wide base of falling water. A small pool at the base slows the water as it crosses an old logging railroad bed. The water then cascades another 10 feet to join Big Creek.

The headwaters of Mouse Creek are high on the slopes of Mount Sterling (5,842 feet in elevation) which has one of the few remaining fire towers in the park. A bench on the banks of Big Creek, opposite Mouse Creek Falls, provides a good place to enjoy the play of water as it bounds down the rocks. Near the top of the cascade water pours into a small hole in such a way that it leaps back into the air. A photo appears on page 57.

To Get There: A 4 mile roundtrip MODERATE hike.

Mouse Creek Falls is 2 miles up the Big Creek Trail which begins near the Big Creek Campground. This moderate walk on a wide road bed gains 500 feet in elevation in the two miles. The trail is open to horses and hikers. In the winter the gate near the ranger station is closed, adding 1.6 miles roundtrip to the walk. On the way up the trail notice the change in rock as you pass over the Greenbrier Fault. The rock changes from the more stratified Rich Butt Sandstone to the more solid Thunderhead Sandstone. Also, stop at Midnight Hole (see above) at 1.4 miles.

Gunter Fork
- •2 Cascades •30 Foot Drop
- •100 Foot Drop/285 Foot Run

Gunter Fork is a major tributary of Big Creek. Named after a family that settled in the mountains of Cocke County, Tennessee and Haywood County, North Carolina, Gunter Fork originates on the northeastern flank of Balsam Mountain between Luftee Knob and Big Cataloochee Mountain.

The first cascade/falls is on the right about 2.1 miles up the Gunter Fork Trail. Gunter Fork splits into two streams as it pours over the exposed sandstone which is inclined from left to right at about 60°. The left stream takes a higher route ending in a 10 foot falls, while the right stream slides down the quartz streaked sandstone at a 45° slant. The water ends in a sizeable plunge pool after falling a total of 30 feet.

Look around the falls. A small cascade tumbles down the steep rock face 40 feet to the right of the falls. In dry weather this small cascade disappears. In wet seasons it puts on a show which rivals the main attraction. Steel cable above the falls is a leftover from earlier logging days.

Only 0.3 mile beyond this cascade is one of the most dramatic falls of water in the park. In a drop of 100 feet in elevation the water of Gunter Fork cascades a distance of 285 feet. It begins as a shallow cascade of 40 feet down an easy slope of 20°. The water then plunges 25 feet straight down in a dazzling falls. From the base of the falls it is 220 feet to a small, shallow pool beside which the trail passes.

The creek is 15 feet wide at the top. After the falls the stream widens as it spreads over an exposed surface of Thunderhead Sandstone which displays many interesting qualities. Near the base of the cascade the rock changes from a knobby conglomerate which resembles cobblestone to a smooth, fine-grained sandstone. The line between these two rock types is well defined, running up from left to right at a 40° angle.

The face of the cascades is sloped like the roof of a house. Do not climb because it can be very dangerous due to wet rocks or ice. The whole scene can be enjoyed from the base where one can listen to the symphony of sounds made by the water and forest. More steel cable ties the present to the logging past.

Though these cascades are far from the roads, they are well worth the effort. The upper cascade is one of the tallest in the Great Smokies.

To Get There: A 16.4 mile roundtrip DIFFICULT hike.

The walk to Gunter Fork is long and wet but rewarding. Walk up the Big Creek Trail 5.8 miles from the Big Creek Campground past Midnight Hole, Mouse Creek Falls, Brakeshoe Springs and Walnut Bottoms (See above for more detailed descriptions). After the Walnut Bottoms back country campsites, the Gunter Fork Trail begins.

At the beginning of the Gunter Fork Trail, Big Creek must be crossed. Except in the driest seasons this is usually a wet crossing. Be careful on the slippery rocks. With high water, the stream may be impassable. Once the crossing of Big Creek is out of the way, Gunter Fork or its tributaries are crossed eight times. This can be done with careful rock hopping.

The first cascade mentioned is 7.9 miles from the Big Creek Campground (2.1 miles from the beginning of the Gunter Fork Trail). The tall upper cascade is 0.3 miles beyond, bringing the entire walk to 8.2 miles. A scenic view of the Gunter Fork/Big Creek valley is 0.3 miles beyond the upper cascade in a small heath bald. The hike to the upper cascade on Gunter Fork is a long 16.4 mile day hike. It's fun to camp in the Walnut Bottom backcountry site, which requires a reservation through the Backcountry Office of the park. The campsite is a very popular one, but enjoyable under the hemlocks beside Big Creek.

The effort that is spent in reaching the upper cascade is well rewarded not just with one of the highest falls of water in the park, but with many scenic falls on the trek up.

<u>Ataga'hi</u>, Gall Place, was believed to be an enchanted lake where animals went to heal their wounds. It was thought to be in the high Smokies west of the headwaters of the Oconaluftee. No one ever saw it, for animals were the only ones who knew its location. If a hunter happened to stray close to the lake he might hear the flap of thousands of wings as many ducks and geese rose into the air. But, when the hunter reached the spot, he would see only a dry spot with no animals, water or grass.

Some said the lake didn't exist. Others thought only a brave who fasted and prayed could sharpen his spiritual vision enough to see it. To one who watched and fasted through the night the lake could be seen in the early morning light as a wide, shallow, purple-blue sheet of water. All types of fish and reptiles lived in the water. Flocks of ducks swam on its surface, birds flew overhead and deer and bear tracks marked its shores. The lake was kept secret from hunters because of the richness of the game.

- A Cherokee Legend

Cosby

Cosby is 19 miles east of Gatlinburg on Highway 321 and 8 miles from I-40 on the Foothills Parkway. The Cosby Campground road begins 1.5 miles from the intersection of Highway 321 with Highway 32. It's 2 miles from Highway 32 to the Cosby Campground and Picnic Area. The campground and picnic areas are rarely crowded even in peak season. A map of the Cosby area is on page 77.

Hen Wallow Falls
•Cascade   •95 Foot Drop

Hen Wallow Falls is a cascade 95 feet high. The water of Hen Wallow Creek slides down gray quartz-streaked sandstone of the Roaring Fork Formation. In drier weather, the cascade begins as two streams of water 6 feet apart and quickly merges to form a thirty foot stream at the base. Wetter weather enlarges the size and force considerably.

It's said that one origin of the name "Hen Wallow" is that ruffed grouse wallowed in the dust near here. The grouse, called "wood hen" by some, is known to engage in such behavior. Carson Brewer offers a more interesting explanation. He writes that Hen Wallow was the name one community gave to another after the first community had been dubbed Roostertown. The names were based on a feud between communities.

Although this cascade doesn't carry a high volume of water, it's a pretty sight any time of year. It's one of the tallest in the park at nearly 100 feet.

To Get There: A 4.2 mile roundtrip MODERATE hike.

The trailhead is 2 miles from Highway 32 near the entrance to Cosby Campground. Begin the hike on the Gabes Mountain Trail across the road from the picnic area. The first part of the hike is on a rocky roadbed which goes 0.3 miles until a feeder trail from the Cosby Campground enters from the left. Stay to the right to cross Rock Creek on a footlog. A log bench provides an opportunity to enjoy the song of the creek.

At 1.1 miles a stone footbridge crosses Crying Creek onto an old roadbed. After 30 yards continue on the Gabes Mountain Trail to the left. Crying Creek is named because a man mistakenly shot his brother in the darkness and confusion of a bear hunt. The trail meanders around the northeastern slopes of Gabes Mountain. After 0.75 miles a modest branch flows under the trail forming a small waterfall of 6 to 8 feet. It's particularly pretty in the winter with no undergrowth and plenty of rain.

One fourth mile from the branch and 2 miles from the beginning is the 700 foot side trail to the base of Hen Wallow Falls. Continue on 140 yards to the top of the falls. **Observe the Warning Signs!** <u>**DO NOT CLIMB ON THE ROCKS!**</u> The view to the north (away from the falls) is of Round and Green Mountains. Cosby can be seen in the distance.

This is a very enjoyable hike anytime of the year. It's a cool spot in the summer or colorful in the fall.

The animals had a disagreement over which had the best coat of fur. It was finally decided to hold a council to determine the finest coat. The talk was that Otter had the finest coat of all but since he lived far up the creek no one could remember exactly what it looked like. Rabbit, fearing that Otter would win and wishing the prize for himself, made a plan to trick Otter out of his coat.

Rabbit through clever questions figured out on which trail Otter would travel to the council. Rabbit made his way up the trail for four days. On the fourth day he met Otter and knew that his coat of soft brown fur was the finest of all. He explained to Otter that he'd been sent to guide Otter to the council.

On the first night Rabbit picked a camping spot. He made comfortable places for the two to sleep. The next day the two traveled on. Near the end of the second day's travel Rabbit began picking up wood and bark. When asked what he was doing the Rabbit replied that he was gathering supplies to keep them warm and comfortable.

After supper Rabbit took a branch and carved it into a paddle. "What are you doing?" inquired the Otter.

"I dream good dreams when I sleep with a paddle under my head."

The Rabbit began to clear a path to the river. The Otter again wondered what the Rabbit was doing. This time the Rabbit said, "This is called Di'tatlaski'yi, that is The Place Where It Rains Fire, because it sometimes rains fire here. In fact, the sky looks a little like it might do so tonight. I'll sit up and watch while you rest. If the fire does come, I'll shout a warning so that you can seek safety in the river. Perhaps you should hang your coat over there so it won't get burnt.

When Rabbit was sure that Otter was asleep he filled the paddle with coals from the fire, threw them in the air and cried out, "It's raining fire! It's raining fire!" The hot coals were falling all around Otter when he awoke. "To the river!" shouted Rabbit. Otter jumped up and raced to the river where he has lived ever since. *- A Cherokee Legend*

Hen Wallow Falls ▲

Gatlinburg - Mt. LeConte

Gatlinburg, the northern gateway to the Smokies is a popular tourist spot with many shops and attractions. The Gatlinburg Craftsman Loop is east of the town off Highway 321 on the way to Cosby. The Sugarlands Visitor Center is 2 miles from Gatlinburg on Highways 441 and 73. A museum and movie are part of the services available at the center which is next to the park headquarters.

From Interstate 40 take Highway 66 to Sevierville, Pigeon Forge and Gatlinburg. Highway 73 brings you to Gatlinburg from Cosby or Townsend., while Highway 441 is an alternate way from Knoxville. The bypass from Pigeon Forge to Sugarlands around Gatlinburg has scenic overlooks of Gatlinburg and Mt. LeConte. This route is a real time saver during peak tourist season. See the map on page 76.

Mt. LeConte, a popular hiking destination, is the third highest peak (6,593 ft.) in the park. Two trails up LeConte, Trillium Gap and Rainbow Falls, have spectacular waterfalls.

The Roaring Fork Motor Trail is a wonderful drive, offering four falls and Roaring Fork itself which is one of the steepest gradients for water in the park. Cataract Falls near the Sugarlands Visitor Center is easily accessible.

Ramsay Cascade
•Cascade   •105 Foot Drop / 122 Foot Run

Ramsay Cascade is one of the most beautiful falls of water in the park. It's also one of the highest at 105 feet in height. The cascade provides the best show in the wetter seasons of winter and spring. However, since the headwaters of Ramsay Prong are high up on the sides of Mt. Guyot, the second highest peak in the park at 6,621 ft., any season has a good flow and thus is picturesque.

The water of Ramsay Prong falls over a jumble of Thunderhead Sandstone. This is the same type of boulder that litters the woods on the trail to Ramsay Cascade. Notice that the sandstone is inclined 30° away from an observer at the base. The constant flow has smoothed the rocks to rounded shapes. The boulders farther from the creek are more angular.

At the top of the cascade, Ramsay Prong is separated into two streams by large boulders with rhododendron growing on them. The stream on the left is the larger of the two. The water hits many outcroppings as it drops 85 feet to a large ledge which is 70 feet across and 25 feet wide. Several pools spread and redirect the stream's flow. Notice how the water has worn the surface of the sandstone to reveal a different underlying texture.

The water leaves the ledge in a 6 foot wide stream to slide under a large overhanging boulder. This 25 foot slide drops approximately 8 feet to where the water falls 12 feet into another pool. Rhododendron and hemlock form a green frame year round.

We've seen Ramsay Cascade completely frozen over in mid-February. The rocks were covered in ice and snow. Even though no moving water could be seen, it could be heard. One hundred feet below the falls is a scenic crossing of Ramsay Prong. Stop for good photos of the cascade.

The temptation to climb the rocks and boulders at the base and sides of the cascade is strong. This is **VERY DANGEROUS!** A number of people have been killed at this cascade over the years. Enjoy the view from the bottom which is a good spot for a picnic.

Ramsay Cascade and Prong are named for the Ramsay family who lived on Webb Creek and had a hunting cabin on this stream. Over the years the creek and cascade took the name from the people who roamed this area in search of game.

To Get There: An 8 mile roundtrip DIFFICULT hike.

From Gatlinburg go east on Highway 321 toward Cosby. Turn at the Greenbrier sign which is 6 miles from traffic light #3 at the intersection of 321 and 441 in Gatlinburg. Follow the Middle Prong of the Little Pigeon River for 3.2 miles. Make a left turn over the wooden bridge. The road dead ends at the trailhead 1.5 miles from the turn.

After the parking area, the trail turns left and crosses a wooden foot bridge. The trail passes through several boulder fields which were probably formed 10,000 to 12,000 years ago. The trail crosses Ramsay Branch on another footbridge. At 1.5 miles the old gravel road ends in a loop.

Continue straight ahead on the foot trail which climbs gradually through rhododendron, large hemlocks and poplars. At 2.2 miles the trail descends to a footlog, then turns left through some large trees. This virgin forest contains silverbell, sweet birch and yellow poplar which are enormous. The trail levels off for 0.25 miles before climbing again. At 2.7

miles is an easy access to the creek which is a good spot to rest before ascending again.

At 2.9 miles, after another footlog, the trail occasionally climbs rock steps as the cascade is approached. Take extra care when crossing the stream because wet rocks can be slippery and unsteady. Return to the parking area by the same route.

The hike to Ramsay Cascade is a full day's walk but worth the time and effort.

Fern Branch Falls
•Cascade   •45 Foot Drop

Fern Branch Falls is a small cascade on the east side of Porters Creek which slips 45 feet over a rock face of Thunderhead Sandstone. Though not a spectacular sight, Fern Branch Falls is a pleasant stopping point on the way up Porters Creek. Water from the small Fern Branch slides down the exposed rock. After a couple of small steps of three to four feet the cascade goes two-thirds of the way to a shelf.

The water then slides to the base over bare stone into rocks and downed trees which litter the base. Wildflowers bloom in abundance in the moist area below the falls. Trillium and white phacelia are especially plentiful. The abundant ferns leave no doubt as to the naming of this branch. Over 65 species of ferns and fern allies thrive in the park.

To Get There: A 3.6 mile roundtrip MODERATE hike.

The trailhead is in the Greenbrier section of the park. Turn off Highway 321 about 6 miles east of Gatlinburg. Pass the Greenbrier Ranger Station and continue up the gravel road. Do not turn left across the bridge but go past a picnic area and pit toilets on the right. The trailhead is 4 miles from the highway.

It's a 1.8 mile moderate walk on the Porters Creek Trail to reach Fern Branch. The falls are to the left of the trail 0.3 miles after crossing Porters Creek on a footlog. Take advantage of the walk to see some of the Smokies history. The first mile of the walk is on a wide, well maintained road. Rock walls built by those who lived and farmed the area wind through the woods. They still stand, but no longer separate fields or contain livestock.

A small cemetery lies up stone steps 30 yards beyond the first bridge. Original settlers and their grandchildren, who died young, are resting in this secluded spot. David Profitt, a Civil War veteran, lies with Whaleys, Ownbys and Profitts. Most of the dates range from 1900 to 1910.

At the end of the road the Smoky Mountain Hiking Club's cabin is to the right. The club built the cabin in the 1930s of logs from two log cabins on the Whaley homestead. The buildings are now owned and maintained by the park.

The entire walk is very pleasant because it follows Porters Creek, which begins on the side of Mt. LeConte. The drive to the trailhead parallels the Little Pigeon River which has many small falls and cascades.

Rainbow Falls
- Falls   - 75 Foot Drop

Rainbow Falls is one of the few actual falls in the park. LeConte Creek free falls 75 feet from a double ledge of gray Thunderhead Sandstone to the rocks below. The water rushes quickly on down the mountainside in small cascades. The first cascade at the base of the falls is 8 to 10 feet.

Rainbow Falls is a tremendous sight in the wettest parts of the year with the swollen creek pounding the rocks at the base. Normally the width of the stream is 6 feet at the top and 15 to 20 feet at the base. A footlog below the 75 foot falls provides a good view. The afternoon sun can produce a rainbow effect, thus the name.

In the winter, ice from the spray transforms the trail, rocks, and bridge into a beautiful but dangerous sight. Prolonged cold can cause ice to build up from the bottom and down from the top to form a column of ice. Although rare, it's most impressive.

It's a nice cool spot in the summer as a way station to LeConte's summit. Spring's wildflowers are plentiful while fall presents a different spectrum of colors. Remember that water flow depends on rainfall, so it can be a trickle or a torrent. Many large hemlock and rhododendron thickets border the creek.

To Get There: A 5.4 mile roundtrip MODERATE-DIFFICULT hike.

In Gatlinburg on Highway 441 turn onto Airport Road at light #8. At 2.6 miles from the light pass the Noah "Bud" Ogle Nature Trail. Beyond the Ogle Place where the road divides, take the right fork. At 3.4 miles park at the Rainbow Falls - Bullhead Trails parking lot. The multiple-use Rainbow Falls Trail goes 2.7 miles to Rainbow Falls on its way to the top of Mt. LeConte (6.6 miles). The trail follows LeConte Creek up to the falls. One is never far from the sound of the mountain stream which falls from high up the slopes of Mt. LeConte toward its union with the Little Pigeon River in Gatlinburg. This creek was once known as Mill Creek because it had 14 tub mills similar to the one at the Noah "Bud" Ogle place. The remains of a cabin are beside the creek at about 0.25 miles from the beginning. This could have been the site of one of the many mills on the creek.

At a switchback is an overlook with views of Sevier County to the north. The first of two footlogs is crossed approximately half way up. About 0.3 miles from Rainbow Falls is an 8 foot waterfall on the right. The trail is heavily used and often crowded. Sometimes parking can be a problem. Get an early start to see this wonder.

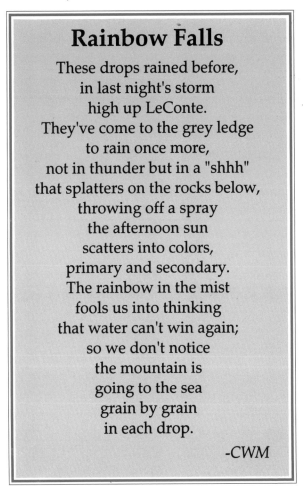

Rainbow Falls

These drops rained before,
in last night's storm
high up LeConte.
They've come to the grey ledge
to rain once more,
not in thunder but in a "shhh"
that splatters on the rocks below,
throwing off a spray
the afternoon sun
scatters into colors,
primary and secondary.
The rainbow in the mist
fools us into thinking
that water can't win again;
so we don't notice
the mountain is
going to the sea
grain by grain
in each drop.

-CWM

Baskins Creek Falls

- Falls   - 35 Foot Drop

Near a grassy open area where a pile of rocks marks an old house site, Falls Branch does a two step off a sandstone ledge. The first step is 20 feet to a 3 foot shelf with the second step another 15 feet to the rocky bottom. This beautiful falls gets little publicity. The trail is rarely traveled.

The waterfall begins as five foot wide Falls Branch drops onto a ledge which funnels the water through a two foot opening. The creek runs off to the left with no pool at the base of the falls. 150 feet below the falls the creek tumbles another 6 feet to a small pool before rushing to its union with Baskins Creek and to downtown Gatlinburg.

The Roaring Fork Sandstone, which forms the cliff, exhibits several geological structures. To the left of the falls verticle fractures known as joints can be seen in the rock. A layering effect can be seen to the right of the waterfall.

Observe the hemlock to the right of the falls' top which bends out over the cliff. Also to the right, about 100 feet is a wet weather falls. We've noticed dirt dauber's nests stuck to the side of the cliff. The mud is from the creek below.

The large boulder at the base of the falls may have fallen from the cliff at the spot where the falls now flow. The downed trees, rocks and boulders point to the ever changing effect of moving water shaping mountains and valleys.

A nice side trip which will extend the walk only 0.75 miles is to Baskins Cemetery and Falls Branch Cascade. After returning to the trail junction at the house site, turn right. A sign points to the side trail up the ridge to the small Baskins Cemetery. Most of the tombstones have no writing but a few tell of deaths around the turn of the century.

Return to the main trail and continue right just a little farther to observe Falls Branch Cascade tripping and trickling off Piney Mountain. The branch isn't wide but makes a long, thin cascade beside the trail for nearly a quarter of a mile.

Baskins Creek gets its name from a man called Bearskin Joe who lived nearby and was noted for his prowess as a hunter, especially of bear. The creek was called Bearskin Joe's Creek which later became Bearskin Creek. This name was eventually misunderstood and shortened to Baskins Creek.

To Get There: A 3 mile roundtrip MODERATE hike.

From Gatlinburg's main street (Highway 441) turn onto Airport Road at light #8. At 2.6 miles from the light pass the Noah "Bud" Ogle Nature Trail. Beyond the Ogle Place where the road divides, take the right fork. At 3.4 miles pass the Rainbow Falls - Bullhead trailheads which lead to Mt. LeConte. At 3.7 miles turn right onto the <u>ONE-WAY</u> Roaring Fork Auto Trail (booklet at the gate). NOTE: The Roaring Fork Auto Trail is closed in the winter. Three miles from the gate (6.7 miles from Gatlinburg) the trail begins at a parking area on the left. A sign for a cemetery stands at the edge of the parking lot.

The Jim Bales place is just over Roaring Fork Creek from the parking lot. Walk to the cemetery which has recently been restored. The many graves are of the Bales and Ogle families. The cemetery is a reminder of previous inhabitants of the area and the difficulty of their lives.

The trail climbs over a ridge where clay soil supports pine and mountain laurel. A long descent on the other side follows an old mountain road through hemlock and rhododendron. Take care not to miss the trail as it turns left to cross Baskin Creek instead of continuing down the old roadbed. After another short ascent, descend to an open area that was a farm. The trail to the falls turns off to the right following Falls Branch to the right.

The return trip is mostly uphill. You can go back the way you came or can continue on the trail over the ridge to the beginning of the Roaring Fork Trail. In the winter the only way to reach the falls is by parking at the beginning of the Roaring Fork Auto Trail and walking up the road 250 yards to the trailhead on the left. No sign marks this end of the path. This is reverse to the trail described above but is a very pleasant walk with about the same distance.

> "There was only the sound of water hurrying over pebbles to an unknown destination -- water that made a tumult drowning the sound of human voices."
>
> *- Loren Eiseley in "Man in the Autumn Light"*

Grotto Falls

Grotto Falls

- Falls   • 25 Foot Drop

Grotto Falls is named for the cave-like appearance of the rocks behind the falls. The water of Roaring Fork free-falls 18 feet after a short 7 foot cascade at the top. The falls spread to a 12 foot width from its 2 foot beginning in the sandstone above. It's fun to walk on the trail behind the waterfall and is the easiest way to get to the other side.

The 20 by 30 foot pool at the base of the falls is a favorite spot to cool hot feet. In its chilly waters many salamanders can be found. Over 22 species of salamanders live in the Smokies. More varieties of salamanders live in the park than in any area of comparable size in the world.

Roaring Fork is said to be one of the steepest creeks in the eastern United States. It loses one mile in elevation from its source near the top of Mt. LeConte to its mouth in Gatlinburg. A 6 foot cascade spills from the pool at Grotto's base. A double falls (4 and 12 feet) with a deep clear green pool is 100 yards below Grotto.

Notice the difference in the rocks around the falls. The dark shale below the falls is softer and thus more easily worn than the harder sandstone above and behind the falls. The Greenbrier Fault is on the trail to the falls. At Grotto, Thunderhead Sandstone is the more resistant rock above the falls with a silty layer of Elkmont Sandstone below.

The Grotto Falls Trail is a good complement to the Roaring Fork Auto Tour with its scenic views and historic buildings. A full day could include Rainbow and Grotto Falls and the Place of A Thousand Drips.

To Get There: A 3 mile roundtrip MODERATE hike.

From Gatlinburg's main street (Highway 441) turn onto Airport Road at light #8. At 2.6 miles from the light pass the Noah "Bud" Ogle Nature Trail. Beyond the Ogle Place where the road divides, take the right fork. At 3.4 miles pass the Rainbow Falls - Bullhead trailheads which lead to Mt. LeConte. At 3.7 miles turn right onto the ONE -WAY Roaring Fork Auto Trail (booklet at the gate). NOTE: The Roaring Fork Auto Trail is closed in the winter. Two miles from the gate (5.7 miles from Gatlinburg) the Grotto Falls Trail begins on the right beyond a parking lot.

The trail begins in a hemlock forest which gives way to yellow poplar and yellow buckeye. Small streams have to be crossed, but pose no problem except in the rainiest seasons. Trillium, violets and spring beauty flourish in late April and early May. Grotto Falls is 1.5 miles from the parking area. Trillium Gap is 1.5 miles beyond the falls. From the gap, it's an easy walk to Brushy Mountain, a heath bald with beautiful views of Greenbrier, Mt. LeConte and Pigeon Forge. It's 3.6 miles from Trillium Gap to the top of Mt. LeConte.

Place of A Thousand Drips
•Cascades   •80 Foot Drop

The Place of A Thousand Drips is well named. Cliff Branch falls 80 feet through many routes before converging with Roaring Fork which rushes by on the opposite side of the road. The single stream spreads to 55 feet wide at the road. Although the water falls 80 feet it travels much farther over the slightly slanted (about 15°) Thunderhead Sandstone. Several streamlets fall 10 and 20 feet at a time.

The Place of A Thousand Drips is a multi-faceted diamond with many surprises of light and water when viewed from various angles. Walk around to fully enjoy this jewel of the Smokies. Thousands upon thousands of years from now a small canyon will be here but for now the small trickles of water work away. The talus to the right of the falls is evidence of the changing nature of the area.

Ferns and moss make this a lush, green location. Hemlocks shade this area which is already cool due to evaporation. Sit on the small bench at the base of the massive sandstone cliff to listen to Roaring Fork and Thousand Drips.

To Get There: Roadside.

A pulloff at 4.9 miles on the Roaring Fork Auto Tour is the place to park. The auto tour is a 5.5 mile one lane paved road beginning at the upper end of the Cherokee Orchard Road 3.7 miles from traffic light #8 in Gatlinburg. Another beautiful site is a 65 foot falls on the left at 4.8 miles. Parking is not readily available here. It's best to walk back from Thousand Drips. Note - The Roaring Fork Auto Tour is closed in the winter.

▲ *Cataract Falls*

Cataract Falls

• Cascade   • 40 Foot Drop

Cataract Falls is a narrow cascade that slides 40 feet down a rocky face before Cataract Branch joins Fighting Creek. Though small, Cataract is easily reached from the Sugarlands Visitor Center.

To Get There: A 0.5 mile EASY walk.

Begin at the Sugarlands Guided Nature Trail behind the Sugarlands Visitor Center. Take the right trail at the fork. Walk to the Park Headquarters building. After passing in front of Park Headquarters turn left on the sidewalk at the parking area. Continue 150 yards to the road. Make another left on the road behind Park Headquarters. The trail begins on the right after the bridge beyond the employee parking area. It's an easy 225 yard walk beside Fighting Creek to Cataract Falls.

The Sinks

• Cascade   • 12 Foot Drop

The Little River sinks suddenly and dramatically over tilted formations of Thunderhead Sandstone. The river is 70 feet wide with a large flow of water. The cascade more than makes up in volume for what it lacks in height. A large, deep plunge pool at the base of The Sinks is a beautiful sight any time of the year.

Highway 73 (Little River Road) follows the railroad bed of the Little River Railroad from Townsend to Elkmont. The Little River Lumber Company constructed the railway to haul lumber from its vast lumber operation in the Smokies. In addition to hauling cut trees from the Smokies' virgin forest, it carried visitors on excursion and "mixed" (that is - tourists and lumber) runs. Daily service from Knoxville to Elkmont was begun in 1909 and continued until 1925 when the line closed. The cut through the rocks near The Sinks was originally for the railroad.

To Get There: Roadside.

The Sinks is below a bridge between Gatlinburg and Townsend on Highway 73 (The Little River Road) 12 miles from the Sugarlands Visitor Center and 6 miles from the intersection of Highway 73 with the Laurel Creek Road at the Townsend Wye.

Laurel Falls

•Cascade   •85 Foot Drop/90 Foot Run

Laurel Falls is a heavily visited falls. It is unusual in that the trail divides the falls into two nearly equal parts. Laurel Branch begins high atop Cove Mountain and flows through virgin forest before arriving at the sandstone ledges of Thunderhead Formation to stairstep its way toward the Little River.

Laurel Branch slides 20 feet before it scatters across the rocky cliff face to fall 30 feet more. The first ledge is 14 feet wide and tilted 30° to the right. The water falls another 16 feet to the trail ledge which is 38 feet from front to back and 45 feet across. Several large stones have been strategically placed for easy crossing of the creek. This is a favorite resting spot for hikers. The boulders around the pool and several pockets in the smooth sandstone are perfect for cooling hot feet in the summer.

The creek falls off the ledge over which the trail passes 22 feet to another ledge (10 feet). The water slips to the right to form a 12 foot wide stream which drops another 12 feet to a last ledge. The final 5 foot fall ends in a pool. The section of the falls below the trail rivals that above. Enjoy the entire display.

Early settlers called rhododendron "laurel". It's no mystery why this area was known as Laurel Branch and Falls. This lovely spot is very popular and often crowded. Try to catch it in the off season or early in the morning.

To Get There: A 2.6 mile roundtrip MODERATE walk.

The trailhead is at Fighting Creek Gap on the Little River Road. It's 3.8 miles west of Sugarlands Visitor Center and 14 miles east of Townsend. Parking is available on both sides of the road. The 1.3 mile paved trail to Laurel Falls is a self-guided nature trail. A leaflet describing noteworthy trail features can be obtained for a small charge at the trailhead.

The trail climbs through oak and hemlock with views of Meigs and Blanket Mountains to the southwest. In mid-May the mountain laurel blooms abundantly in a wonderful show of white and pink. Steep cliffs of Thunderhead Sandstone are reached before the falls. Return to the parking area by the same route.

A longer walk to the Cove Mountain firetower can be made by continuing 2.5 miles on the trail beyond the falls. The trail passes through beautiful virgin forest. Allow plenty of time for this 8 mile roundtrip hike.

Laurel Falls ▲

Meigs Falls ▲

Huskey Branch Falls
•Cascade   •50 Foot Drop/120 Foot Run

Huskey Branch is a pleasant stream which slides down bare sandstone into the Little River. The cascade begins as an 8 foot falls before traveling 110 feet to the river. Though not as steep as many other cascades, it has a beauty of its own especially when the rhododendron are in bloom.

Notice the shaley siltstone at the top left of the falls. It is more easily worn than the quartz-streaked sandstone. Thus the cascade starts its journey to the river through the channel once occupied by the siltstone.

The Huskey name is associated with this area of the Smokies because several Huskey families lived in Sugarlands. Sam Huskey had a store in the Sugarlands. Huskey Gap and Branch take their names from these who lived and hunted this region.

Sit on the bench to enjoy a picnic or the sound of the water. The cascade passes under a bridge on the Little River Trail. A large, deep pool in the Little River is at the base of the cascade. The Little River splashes and tumbles over many rocks and boulders as it falls from its headwaters high up the sides of Clingmans Dome, the highest peak in the Smokies.

To Get There: A 2 mile roundtrip EASY walk.

Take Little River Road five miles from Sugarlands Visitor Center toward Townsend. Turn into the Elkmont area and pass the campground by turning left. Continue to the left at another intersection. Park at the turnaround which is 3 miles from Little River Road.

The Little River Trail is an easy one that parallels the river on an old road bed. Benches along the way provide nice opportunities to enjoy the river. Icicles cling to the rocky cliffs on the right of the trail in the winter. Wildflowers abound in the spring and summer. Fall's show of color is particularly pretty in this hardwood forest.

"Tis the rocks in the stream that make the brook sing."
- An old mountain saying.

Meigs Falls

- Falls
- 28 Foot Drop

Several small tributaries converge on the northern slo[pe] Mountain to form Meigs Creek, which flows through a gorge Little River at Highway 73. The falls begin with two modest steps of 5 feet and 2 feet when Meigs Creek emerges from a tunnel of dense rhododendron, hardwoods and pine. The creek travels 45 feet from the top steps to drop 5 feet into a 3 foot wide gutter which shifts the flow from right to left about 15 feet. The water then plunges 28 feet over exposed Thunderhead Sandstone to form a beautiful sight which can be seen from the road.

The creek spreads from 12 to 16 feet until the water hits a ledge which further spreads the water to 30 feet. On this ledge the water shifts back to the right. The creek steps down a couple more ledges before going 125 feet to join the Little River.

Meigs Mountain, Creek and Falls are named after Col. Return Jonathan Meigs (1734-1823) who acted as U.S. agent to the Cherokee from 1801 to 1823. After serving with distinction in the Revolutionary War, Meigs moved to Ohio from his home in Connecticut. He was appointed as the Indian agent to assist in civilizing the Cherokee and to convince them to move west of the Mississippi River.

In 1802, Meigs surveyed the boundary between land the Cherokee ceded to the settlers in a treaty. The line ran from the top of Chilhowee Mountain to the crest of the Smokies. It was difficult to sight the line due to the dense growth and steep ridges. At one point a large blanket was put on a pole so that it could be spotted. Meigs Mountain is north of Blanket Mountain along the surveyed line.

Meigs suggested that land be given to individual Cherokee and that each should be granted citizenship. The states reacted vehemently to this proposal which was before its time. Meigs' name on the map attests to Return Jonathan Meigs' service to Cherokee and settlers alike.

Near Meigs Falls was a swinging railroad bridge which went from cliff top to near the Little River with no support underneath the bridge. This bridge was used in the early 1900s in the logging operations of the area.

To Get There: Roadside

Meigs Falls is on the south side of Little River Road 13 miles from Sugarland Visitor Center and 5 miles from the intersection of Highway

the Laurel Creek Road near Townsend. The Sinks are about 1
on the Gatlinburg side of Meigs Falls.

Enjoy Meigs Falls from the pull-off, which is a great vantage point for photographs. No trail goes to the falls.

▲ *Spruce Flats Falls*

Middle Prong of the Little River below Lynn Camp Prong ▲

Cades Cove - Townsend

Cades Cove is a picturesque mountain valley in the western part of the park. Its popularity is due to outstanding scenery and plentiful wildlife. The 11 mile loop is a popular auto trail especially in the fall. The Cades Cove Visitor Center at Cable Mill is half way around the one-way loop.

Townsend, once a logging center, is a small town at the western entrance to the Great Smoky Mountains National Park. Townsend can be reached via Highway 321 - 20 miles south of Maryville and 15 miles southwest of Pigeon Forge. From Gatlinburg take Highway 73 eighteen miles to the "Wye" which is an intersection of roads and rivers that is very popular. It's only 7 more miles from the "Wye" to Cades Cove.

The two-way Laurel Creek Road is the only entrance into Cades Cove. Two additional exits leaving the cove are both one-way gravel roads. The Rich Mountain Road goes over Rich Mountain to Townsend and the Parsons Branch Road traverses Hannah Mountain to Highway 129 at Chilhowee Lake. Both are closed in the winter.

Parsons Branch Road follows and crosses Parsons Branch. The road reaches its highest point at Sams Gap after which it descends beside Parsons Branch with numerous fords to splash through. Just remember it's a long way back to Maryville or the park via the Foothills Parkway.

The Rich Mountain Road, a drier route with scenic overlooks, traverses Rich Mountain into Tuckaleechee Cove and Townsend. Allow plenty of time for both roads. On days when Cades Cove is jammed with traffic, Rich Mountain and Parsons Branch afford nice escapes.

Many falls are in the Cades Cove - Townsend area; from the scenic Spruce Flats Falls at Tremont to the popular Abrams Falls in Cades Cove. A map of the area is on page 76.

Spruce Flats Falls (Three Step Falls)
•4 Cascades   •125 Foot Drop/320 Foot Run

The cascades are near the confluence of Spruce Flats Branch with the Middle Prong of the Little River. The falls have been called Three Step Falls because only three can be seen from a vantage point at the base. However, a fourth cascade is 75 feet above the third one. It is beautiful as the water of Spruce Flats Creek drops 28 feet into a trough which pushes the water to the left.

The third cascade is the smallest at 17 feet. Only 20 feet separate the base of the upper cascade from the top of the middle one, which is 28 feet tall. The creek moves 100 feet before falling over the last, lowest and largest cascade which is 60 feet tall and 60 feet wide. A large plunge pool holds the water only temporarily before it falls on down to the Little River. In the winter the Little River and the road can be seen from near the cascades.

Thunderhead Sandstone, which is resistant to erosion and is streaked with quartz, makes up the cliffs at the falls. The Oconaluftee Fault runs nearby on its way to Cherokee from Cades Cove. Notice that the rocks on the left side of the falls are more rounded than the jumble of rocks on the slope to the right. The more angular stones were chipped and blasted from the cliffs to build a logging railroad bed which is about 100 feet above the lowest falls.

This area was one of the last logged by the Little River Logging Company. Early efforts by loggers to cut timber near here were thwarted by Will Walker who, in 1859, settled the flat area where the Great Smoky Mountain Institute now stands. Walker didn't sell the timber rights to the area until just before his death in 1920.

These cascades are used for work at the Great Smoky Mountains Institute in its environmental education efforts. The trail is well traveled but not crowded. This is actually an undiscovered jewel in the park.

To Get There: A 2 mile roundtrip MODERATE hike.

From the intersection of Highway 73 (Little River Road) and Laurel Creek Road, go 0.2 miles toward Cades Cove (west) and turn at the Tremont sign. Follow the Tremont Road 2 miles to the Great Smoky Mountains Institute which is on the left across the Middle Prong of the Little River. Turn left and cross the bridge to park at the Institute parking lot. The office has a sales area, resource center and restrooms.

Walk on the road from the parking lot to the employee housing beyond the Institute buildings to a path that is marked "Falls." After 30 feet the trail turns left and climbs the side of the ridge past the water tank for the Institute. Several signs mark the way. The trail is high above the Middle Prong of the Little River (sometimes more than 300 feet). A couple of wet weather branches that drain the steep slopes of Mill Ridge are crossed. The first part of the trail is steep but soon moderates.

Lynn Camp Prong Cascade
•Numerous Cascades & Falls

A sandstone cliff provides an excellent overlook of the water of Lynn Camp Prong as it rushes down a rocky chute. The creek is 10 feet wide with a good flow at the head of the upper cascade which is 35 feet long. After spreading to 20 feet the water travels 85 feet to a 4 foot ledge. At the base of the cliff and the small ledge, the creek slides to the left in a small 3 foot channel for 80 feet. It then shoots down a bare rock face in a narrow stream for 55 feet where it hits a rock shelf and splashes into the air. A plunge pool at the foot catches the airborne water 10 feet after its launch.

A large gray rock face of Thunderhead Sandstone slants at about 40° making it easy to climb on. The creek is forced into such a narrow confine that it has much power causing it to leap into the air near the base. The drop of the falls is 65 feet from the first cascade to the plunge pool.

Sixty paces beyond the second bench is an 8 foot waterfall. Look for an old steel cable which is left from logging days. Below the small upper falls is a wonderful place to cool hot feet.

▲ *Lynn Camp Prong Cascade*

Indian Flats Falls ▲

Another set of cascades is 0.25 miles up the Middle Prong Trail. Two groups of falls form these beautiful cascades. The first group is two falls of 4 and 6 feet. On the 6 foot step the stream splits into three falls. The rocks are moss-covered with rhododendron, beech and doghobble on the banks. A bench is near the upper group made up of a 2 foot and 6 foot falls which is one hundred feet upstream.

A Civilian Conservation Corps camp occupied an area up the road from this cascade in the early 1930s. The name Lynn Camp, perhaps, comes from the many Linwood (basswood) trees in the area. Or it may come from the Scotch-Irish who settled the mountains. A lin (or linn) is a small pool in a creek at the base or top of a waterfall. This creek has many a beautiful lin.

To Get There: A 1 mile roundtrip EASY walk.

From the intersection of Highway 73 and Laurel Creek Road go 0.2 miles toward Cades Cove (west) and turn left at the Tremont sign. Follow Tremont Road 2 miles past the ranger's house to the Great Smoky Mountains Institute. On the right a booklet for the Tremont Logging History Auto Tour can be purchased for a small charge. Follow the gravel road 3 miles until it ends at a turnaround.

Cross the foot bridge over Lynn Camp Prong to an old railroad bed which goes in two directions. To the right a Quiet Walkway follows the old bed 0.25 miles to a bridge. However, take the left fork which follows the creek along the Middle Prong Trail. The trail is a gravel roadbed which is open to horses.

After 0.3 miles a bench on the left has a good view of a large cascade. Go to the second bench which overlooks the middle of the cascade. The 8 foot falls is 60 paces beyond the bench between rhododendron and a large rock. Continue 0.25 miles upstream past a rock cliff on the right of the trail and around a bend to the upper set of cascades. A bench is at the top of these.

The Middle Prong Trail changes to the Greenbrier Ridge Trail before it reaches the Appalachian Trail 7.5 miles away. This walk is fun combined with the Auto Trail and the Spruce Flats Falls Trail or as a nice side visit on the way to Cades Cove.

Indian Flats Falls
- 4 Falls
- 65 Foot Drop/170 Foot Run

Indian Flats Falls is a strand of four falls whose individual beauty is magnified due to their placement on the necklace of Indian Flats Prong. When viewed from the base, Indian Flats Falls is a truly magnificent sight but each step has a wonder of its own.

The headwaters of Indian Flats Prong are near the crest of the Smokies at Mt. Davis, Hemlock Knob and Miry Ridge. The water, cooled by the high elevation, quickly tumbles to the falls. The trail arrives at the base of the uppermost falls which drops 20 feet in three streams into a small pool. The creek travels to the right around an island of rounded stones for 60 feet to the next ledge which is 35 feet wide.

The second step begins with the creek at a width of 10 feet but this spreads to 16 feet when the water strikes a small ledge partway down the 18 foot fall. A large circular pool is at the base of the second falls. The Thunderhead Sandstone of the area is scoured clean and smooth with pockets of rounded rocks. Tilting only slightly away from the viewer, the sandstone forms the numerous ledges of the falls. The creek moves 45 more feet then drops off the third ledge. The third step is the smallest at 9 feet.

The fourth and final step is 18 feet beyond the third. The water falls 12 more feet before being squeezed back to normal creek size by boulders at the base. Round holes with chucks of quartz and other rocks resemble baskets of eggs. The rocks combine with the swirling action of the water to carve out the holes.

Thick rhododendron crowds both sides of the stream. Doghobble, trillium and hardwoods also populate the forest. Lush moss covers the rocks and ledges to form a green tapestry interwoven with bluets and trillium in the spring. Indian Flats Falls is definitely worth the trek.

To Get There: A 7.5 mile roundtrip MODERATE hike.

From the intersection of Little River Road and Laurel Creek Road go 0.2 miles toward Cades Cove (west) and turn left at the Tremont sign. Follow Tremont Road 2 miles to the Great Smoky Mountains Institute. On the right a booklet for the Tremont Logging History Auto Tour can be purchased for a small charge. Follow the gravel road 3 miles until it ends at a turnaround.

Cross the footbridge over Lynn Camp Prong to an old railroad bed which goes in two directions. Take the left fork which follows the creek along the Middle Prong Trail. Pass the cascades and falls mentioned above in the Lynn Camp Prong Cascades hike. Stay on the Middle Prong Trail past the trail junction with the Jakes Gap Trail. A little over 1 mile past the trail junction the trail climbs the ridge on a couple of switchbacks. Indian Flats Prong is crossed on a bridge. See the ruins of an old bridge up creek (to the right) of the present bridge.

The trail moves away from the creek and upward on more switchbacks. At the second switchback a side trail leaves the main trail on the right. Follow the side trail on an old road bed about 150 yards to the base of the uppermost falls. The side trail isn't marked and can be overgrown in the summer. It's worth the struggle through the underbrush for this sight. Indian Flats Falls is a good day-long adventure with plenty of opportunities for viewing falls and cascades along Lynn Camp and Indian Flats Prongs.

▲ *An unnamed falls on the Rainbow Falls Trail.*

Abrams Falls ▲

An Early Morning Rainbow at Abrams Falls ▲

Abrams Falls

• Falls   • 25 Foot Drop

The 25 foot high Abrams Falls plunges into a large pool with the volume of a small river rather than a creek. Eighteen creeks and branches flow into Cades Cove to form Abrams Creek which is the only water exit from the cove to the Little Tennessee River. The creek is 35 feet wide at the top of the falls. The plunge pool is over 100 feet long and nearly the same in width. The water is very deep with a dark green color.

The force of the falls throws spray over 50 feet into rhododendron and hemlock on the bank opposite the trail. Spray forms ice on the rocks and plants in the coldest months and cools the air in the hottest. When the early morning sun comes over the ridge and hits the falls, a beautiful rainbow can be seen. One January morning we saw a double rainbow as we stood on the rocks beside the falls. The outer rainbow's colors were in opposite order to the inside one.

Smooth pebbles and large battered logs show the force of the water. The falls thunder over a multi-layered cliff of Cades Sandstone. Above the falls are four or five one foot steps where Abrams Creek drops over more of the sandstone which is prevalent in this area.

Abrams Creek and Falls were probably named for Old Abraham a Cherokee who lived near the cove in Chilhowee. A Cherokee village, Tsiyahi, Otter Place, was in all likelihood named for the otters which once frolicked in the creek. Attempts are being made to reintroduce the otter to the Great Smoky Mountains.

To Get There: A 5 mile roundtrip MODERATE hike.

Take the Cades Cove Loop Road about 5 miles to a right turn after crossing Abrams Creek. Follow the gravel road 0.5 miles to a parking area. Start at the parking area at the junction of Mill and Abrams Creeks. A footbridge crosses Abrams Creek to a trail split. To the right it's 0.5 miles through bottom land to the Elijah Oliver cabin. Straight ahead at the split is the Abrams Creek Trail which goes through a rhododendron tunnel that is especially beautiful in early summer when it's in full bloom.

The trail generally follows the creek until it ascends a pine-covered ridge. Arbutus Branch is crossed before ascending Arbutus Ridge, 200 feet above the creek. At 1 mile the ridge top is gained, then the trail descends through pines and mountain laurel to a footlog over Stony Branch. A third and final ridge is climbed at 2 miles. A footlog across Wilson Creek is reached at 2.5 miles.

A short side trail to the left goes to the top of Abrams Falls. Use caution when at the top. Wet rocks are slippery. The last 0.2 miles down to Wilson Creek and the side trail are steep and narrow.

Return to the parking lot by the same trail. This is a beautiful walk in the spring and summer providing plenty of wildflowers, rhododendron and mountain laurel. This hike goes well with a day trip to Cades Cove. Picnic at the falls or at the Cable Mill Historic Site.

Tips for Waterfall Photography

A picture of a waterfall never measures up to the sight, sound and experience of being there. These suggestions will enhance your efforts to capture some of their beauty.

1. **Film** - Generally, slide film reproduces a scene more accurately than print film. We prefer KodaChrome 25 and 64, and FujiChrome 50 for the fine grain they offer. Fine grain films produce better enlargements.

2. **Exposure** - Slide film isn't as forgiving when it comes to under or overexposure. Bracket your shots, that is, shoot at the correct meter reading then over and under expose by half a stop and then one full stop. When shooting at an eighth of a second or longer water produces a flowing, silky effect. Try to avoid bright, sunny midday shots. Waterfalls reflect much more light than the surrounding forest greenery, therefore making very contrasty pictures. Try early morning and late afternoon as well as overcast days.

3. **Lenses** - Various lenses can be used for waterfall shots. You may wish to use a wide-angle lens to include some of the surrounding area. A telephoto lens may be utilized to isolate a portion of a falls.

4. **Tripod** - If possible, a tripod should be used to insure clear photographs and for slower shutter speeds. Tripods also assist in composing the photograph you want.

Try shooting from different angles and heights around the waterfall to give different perspectives. The best advice is to take more pictures than wanted, so that the scene desired will be in the pictures taken.

Clingmans Dome

Clingmans Dome is the highest peak in the Great Smoky Mountains National Park at 6,641 feet. In spite of its great height, it's the most accessible summit due to a paved road which leads nearly to the top. An observation tower affords fantastic views which are available to everyone who is willing to stroll the 0.5 miles through the spruce-fir forest of the high Smokies. The Appalachian Trail is at its highest point of its entire 2,100 mile length at Clingmans Dome. Not many falls are close to the crest of the Great Smokies. However, Forney Creek Cascade is beautiful.

Turn onto the seven mile Clingmans Dome Road as it leaves Highway 441 at Newfound Gap. This intersection is 27 miles from Cherokee and 22 miles from Gatlinburg. The Clingmans Dome Road is closed in the winter (from Nov. to April). Plenty of parking is available at the Forney Ridge Parking Area. For a map of this area see page 77.

▲ *Hazel Creek Cascade*

Forney Creek Cascade
•Cascade   •85 Foot Drop/245 Foot Run

Forney Creek Cascade is a combination of two slides of water over quartz-streaked sandstone. The water flows through a 2 foot opening in a jumble of rocks, then begins a 110 foot slide down the first incline. The course grained sandstone has been smoothed by the creek. The rock is criss-crossed with quartz streaks 3 to 4 inches thick. The creek quickly spreads to 15 feet then on to 25 feet. The main flow of water stays to the left as it slips into a shallow pool.

The creek narrows to 5 feet before it begins its descent again. This time it slides 135 feet spreading to 55 feet as it enters a shallow pool. The upper slide is steeper than the lower one. A small creek pours into the plunge pool on the right at the base of the cascade. A large rail is twisted in the rocks at the base.

The immediate vicinity of the cascade has been over-used due to illegal camping. The trampled ground and many fire circles show the strain of too many who have abused this scenic spot. Please use care and common sense in visiting.

Forney Creek Cascade ▲

To Get There: A 6 mile DIFFICULT hike

The hike begins at the Forney Ridge Parking Area below Clingmans Dome. Use the Forney Ridge Trail which begins to the left of the paved trail to Clingmans Dome. The Forney Ridge Trail is a rocky walk, so wear good shoes or boots. Descend 0.1 mile to a trail divide. Take the left trail to descend the western slope of Forney Ridge. This is through the spruce-fir forest which is fighting for survival against the balsam wooly adelgid (aphid).

Take the Forney Creek Trail which turns off to the right at 1.1 miles. The Forney Ridge Trail continues straight ahead to Andrews Bald which is about 1 mile from the trail junction. Descend the Forney Creek Trail. The forest opens after a set of switchbacks to reveal sparse undergrowth beneath second growth hardwoods. A forest fire in the 1920s swept this area. A steep graded incline crosses the trail. This was used by the Norwood Lumber Company in its logging operations.

The trail meets a small stream 1.3 miles from the trail intersection. Here the trail follows the creek down the valley toward Forney Creek. After 0.7 miles the trail crosses the upper part of Forney Creek. Rails and other artifacts are scattered about this crossing. The trail stays above the creek for 200 yards before descending to a worn spot caused by illegal camping beside the creek. The cascade is at this over-used area. Backcountry campsite #68 is 0.25 miles below the cascade. The walk back to the parking area is all uphill.

> "I now entered upon the verge of the dark forest, charming solitude! as I advanced through the animating shades, observed on the farther grassy verge a shady grove; thither I directed my steps. On approaching these shades, between stately columns of the superb forest trees, presented to view, rushing from rocky precipices under the shade of the pensile hills, the unparalleled cascade of Falling Creek, rolling and leaping off the rocks: the waters uniting below, spread a broad glittering sheet over a vast convex elevation of plain smooth rocks, and are immediately received by a spacious bason, where trembling in the centre through hurry and agitation, they gently subside, encircling the painted still verge; from whence gliding swiftly, they soon form a delightful little river, which continuing to flow moderately, is restrained for a moment, gently undulating in a little lake: they then pass on rapidly to a high perpendicular steep of rocks, from whence these delightful waters are hurried down with irresistible rapidity. I here seated myself on the moss-clad rocks, under the shade of spreading trees and floriferous fragrant shrubs, in full view of the cascades."
>
> -From _The Travels of William Bartram_ by William Bartram, 1791.

Cherokee - Deep Creek

Oconaluftee means "by the river" in the Cherokee language. The Cherokee - Deep Creek area abounds in water, cascades and falls. Cherokee is on the park's southern boundary at the junction of Highways 441 and 19 about 1-1/2 hours from Gatlinburg. It's in the Qualla Indian Reservation which is the home of the Eastern Band of Cherokees. In the town of Cherokee are numerous opportunities to learn of the Smokies' original native American inhabitants.

The Oconaluftee Visitor Center is at the park's southern entrance on Highway 441 near Cherokee. The Pioneer Homestead is a good interpretation of life in the 1800s, as is nearby Mingus Mill. The southern terminus of the Blue Ridge Parkway is at Cherokee. This national parkway gives access to some of the most beautiful mountain scenery in the eastern United States.

National park campgrounds near Cherokee are Smokemont (on Newfound Gap Road 3.2 miles north of the visitor center), Balsam Mtn. (9 miles off the Blue Ridge Parkway) and Deep Creek (near Bryson City). These three campgrounds usually don't have the crowds of those on the Tennessee side.

The Deep Creek Campground is located north of Bryson City on Deep Creek. Take Highway 19 south 10 miles from Cherokee to Bryson City. Turn onto Everett Street in Bryson City. At .2 miles turn right onto Depot Street then turn left onto Ramseur Street. After another immediate turn to the right the road becomes curvy. Follow the signs to the Deep Creek Campground which is 4 miles from Bryson City.

Four beautiful falls are in the immediate area of the Deep Creek Campground. The creek itself is well named with a large flow of water year round. Horace Kephart, noted writer and early advocate for a national park in the Smokies, last lived at Bryson Place on Deep Creek.

Smokemont Campground is near the junction of Bradley Fork and the Oconaluftee River. It's popular and often crowded, but is open all year, unlike Deep Creek and Balsam Mountain which are closed in the winter. Balsam Mountain is the highest campground in the park. It's perfect for a cool night's camping in the heat of the summer and is a great starting point for a walk to Flat Creek Falls. To reach Balsam Mountain Road drive 11 miles on the Blue Ridge Parkway from Cherokee. Turn onto Balsam Mountain Road. For a map of the area see page 78.

▲ *Midnight Hole*

▲ *Twentymile Creek Cascade*

Mingo Falls ▲

Chasteen Creek
•Cascade   •15 Foot Drop/50 Foot Run

Lying near the Greenbrier Fault, Chasteen Creek Falls is a picturesque cascade in a lovely setting. The small creek slides 50 feet down smoothly worn sandstone. The twenty foot wide stream spreads to nearly twice that width before the banks of the creek at the cascade's base squeeze the water back together. Notice the two inch thick streak of quartz on the large rock at the top left of the cascade. Since the cascade is inclined at only 25°, the fall of the water is not very great.

Large hemlock in a primarily second growth hardwood forest provide a shaded setting for doghobble and rhododendron to grow. Although this cascade doesn't have the dramatic plunge that others have, it's a wonderful spot for a picnic.

Chasteen Creek's headwaters are on the slopes of Hughes and Mine Ridges. The valley formed by the creek is wide and open. Numerous house sites attest to the cultivation and subsequent logging of the area.

To Get There: A 4 mile roundtrip MODERATE hike.

Begin at the north end of the Smokemont Campground on the Bradley Fork Trail. The 1.2 mile walk up the wide road bed to a junction with Chasteen Creek Trail is beside Bradley Fork which is named for early settlers of the area. Several benches are beside the stream.

Turn onto the Chasteen Creek Trail which veers to the right. Soon after the trail intersection is backcountry campsite #50. Continue up Chasteen Creek Trail for 0.8 miles. A foot trail leaves the road on the left at an old horse rack. Take the foot trail around to the cascade. Return by the same route.

Mingo Falls
•Cascade   •180 Foot Drop

This magnificent fall of water actually lies outside the boundaries of the park, within the Qualla Indian Reservation. Since it's included in the park's literature and is the most spectacular sight in the area, it had to be a part of this book.

The water of Mingo Creek drops 180 feet over a bare sandstone ledge which is on the Greenbrier Fault. The rock is highly stratified, slanting down from the left to the right at about 15°. This sandstone is inclined away from the viewer at 45° back into the mountain. The water splashes over hundreds of small shelves.

At the top, the falls begin as an 8 foot wide stream. Tiny streamlets stray off to the right side of the bare rock face while the main force of the water stays to the left. The whole cascade widens to 40 feet at the base.

A bare rock cliff, to the left of the falls, is separated from the creek by pine and mountain laurel. Notice that at the base of the falls the vegetation is mainly rhododendron and hemlock, but at the top it's pine and mountain laurel.

A small bridge and bench provide excellent spots for photographing or simply enjoying the magnificent sight. A trail does go to the top, but the view is not as good as that at the base.

To Get There: A 0.5 mile roundtrip MODERATE walk.

Take the Big Cove Road which begins 2.5 miles south of the Oconaluftee Visitor Center. Go on the Big Cove Road under the Blue Ridge Parkway 5 miles to the Mingo Falls Campground which is on the right. Cross the bridge to the campground. Parking is available to hikers.

The trail begins to the left of the water plant for the campground. The first 200 yards are very steep. Several benches are provided to make the ascent easier. The trail levels off to follow the creek around to the base of the falls.

The trail to the top begins at the top of the steep part which is half way to the base of the falls. It goes up the ridge about 0.25 miles to the head of the falls. After a switchback a small trail veers to the right. Follow this smaller trail away from what appears to be the main trail. This little trail goes to the top where a fence provides moderate protection on the steep, bare rock. **DO NOT FOLLOW OTHER TRAILS DOWN. GO BACK THE WAY YOU CAME.**

This sight is easily reached and should not be missed.

Flat Creek Falls
•Cascade   •200+ Foot Drop

The creek leaves the Flat Creek area to fall over 200 feet off Balsam Mountain in a 20 foot wide stream. The exposed rock over which the water rushes is part of the Thunderhead Formation which is prevalent in

▲ *Flat Creek Falls*

the park. This cascade is such a long one that it is difficult to see the bottom from the top. Mountain laurel overhangs the creek above the falls. The Balsam Mountain Road can be seen in the distance on the side of the mountain across the deep, steep-sided valley.

Pay attention to the sign! <u>**DON'T CLIMB ON THE ROCKS!**</u> It's very dangerous due to wet, slick rocks. Stay to the right of the sign to get to the top of the falls. The small trail to the left of the sign isn't a trail. It's <u>very</u> steep and washed out. No good way to the bottom is available! Enjoy this wonder from the heights of Balsam Mountain. This is one of the highest falls of water in the park.

To Get There: A 2 or 4 Mile Roundtrip Moderate Hike.

Turn onto the Balsam Mountain Road off the Blue Ridge Parkway 11 miles from Cherokee. One route begins on a road bed at the Heintooga Picnic Area beyond the Balsam Mountain Campground. Views to the north and west from the overlook reveal the distant peaks of the high Smokies. Veer to the right off the roadbed onto a foot trail.

The trickle of Flat Creek can be heard after 0.5 miles. The first footlog crosses the upper part of Flat Creek which moves down the gentle slope.

Mouse Creek Falls ▲

At 1.5 miles, a second footlog is soon followed by a third. The 300 yard side trail turns to the right to descend to the top of the cascade. The Flat Creek Trail continues on 1 mile to the road but it's a 3.7 mile walk by road to your car.

However, for a shorter walk to the falls, you can begin on the Balsam Mountain Road 5 miles from the Blue Ridge Parkway. The trailhead is at a pulloff on the left. Descend from the road to Bunches Creek and a footlog. A large hollow tree is at the second footlog. The trail climbs for 0.5 miles to the junction with the side trail to the falls.

Either route is good. Late June is beautiful to visit this higher elevation area for its show of rhododendron, mountain laurel, flame azalea and blackberries. For another treat, drive back to Cherokee on the 28 mile one-way Balsam Mountain Road from Heintooga to Round Bottom and see Mingo Falls. Spring, fall and summer are all wonderful on Balsam Mountain. However, the road is closed in the winter due to snow and ice.

Juneywhank Falls
•Cascade   •80 Foot Drop / 125 Foot Run

A footlog crosses Juneywhank Branch near the middle of this 125 foot cascade. Stand on the log to experience the water all around you. The creek flows through a 3 foot wide opening in the rocks at the top, then spreads to a width of 20 feet at the footlog. The main flow is on the right side with a lesser stream on the left. A thin film of water spreads between the two. The creek narrows to 6 feet as it travels down the ridge.

The first 20 feet is an easy slope before Juneywhank Branch falls 30 feet over Thunderhead Sandstone, which has horizontal streaks of quartz and vertical cracks. The incline is not as steep under the bridge but then drops another 45 feet through rocks and fallen timber. Dead oaks cross the creek at the top of the cascade. The rocks are moss covered and surrounded with doghobble.

The name Juneywhank is an unusual one. It's been said it's Cherokee for "The bear went that-a-way." The Cherokee word for "bear" is "yona" or "juna." However, the more likely explanation is that Junaluska Whank, who was named for the famed Cherokee chief, Junaluska, lived in the area. Junaluska Whank was called Juney by friends and neighbors. He is supposedly buried somewhere near the falls.

A small 20 foot cascade is downstream from the falls. At the cascade is a good view of Juneywhank Falls and Branch. Juneywhank is a wonderful short walk which fits in well with an overnight stay at Deep Creek Campground or a hike to Indian Creek Falls.

To Get There: A 0.5 mile roundtrip EASY walk.

The trail begins before the parking area above the Deep Creek Campground, 0.6 miles from the entrance. The easy stroll through a mostly hardwood forest is a fun way to listen to the many birds. A side trail, 0.25 miles from the beginning, leads to a footlog at the falls. The main trail continues on to the top of Juneywhank Falls. A level open area above the falls marks an old house site. Return by the same route or follow the creek down to the parking lot.

Toms Branch Falls
•Cascade   •80 Foot Drop

Sit on the bench beside Deep Creek opposite Toms Branch Falls to best observe this marvelous cascade. Two small steps at the top begin the more than 80 foot fall into Deep Creek. The water flows over stratified sandstone onto two larger and more widely spaced steps before hitting a last shelf above the rushing creek.

The stream starts on the right, shifts to the left for most of the trip down and then returns to the right before the final shelf divides it into two streams. Toms Branch is 3 feet wide at the head of the cascade, widens to 8 feet in the mid section and spreads to 10 feet at the base.

The name has been difficult to track down. It has been suggested it was named for Tom Wiggins, a settler in the area. Although the name's origin is obscure, the cascade still delights all who walk up the Deep Creek Trail.

To Get There: A 0.5 mile roundtrip EASY walk.

Begin at the parking area 0.6 miles above the entrance to the Deep Creek Campground. Walk up the multi-use graveled jeep road that is the Deep Creek Trail. Toms Branch drops off the ridge on the right side of Deep Creek opposite the trail 0.25 miles from the trailhead.

▲ *Toms Branch Falls*

Indian Creek Falls ▲

Indian Creek Falls
- Cascade   • 25 Foot Drop/45 Foot Run

A large plunge pool is at the base of 45 foot Indian Creek Falls. The water slides down a 45° slope of Thunderhead Sandstone to form a beautiful cascade which is framed by rhododendron. The main flow is on the left with the stream on the right obscured by overhanging vegetation. The 25 foot wide stream broadens to 35 feet at the base.

The jumble of rocks on the right bank comes from the road which is above the falls. A motor trail was to have been constructed, but was later abandoned by the Park Service in order to better preserve the area. Wildflowers and rhododendron bloom in abundance along Indian and Deep Creeks. Sit on the bench above the falls for a good view.

To Get There: A 2 mile roundtrip EASY hike.

The trail begins at the parking area above Deep Creek Campground, 0.6 miles from the entrance. Leave the parking lot on this multiple use trail which is very popular with horse back riders. It's an easy walk beside Deep Creek, a cool spot in the hottest summer months. Toms Branch Falls is on the opposite side of Deep Creek 0.25 miles from the parking area.

Deep Creek is crossed on a wide bridge at 0.3 miles. At the trail divide (0.8 miles) take the right fork up a jeep road a few hundred yards to the small trail which goes off to the left. After returning by the same route, try the short walk to Juneywhank Falls.

Little Creek Falls
- Cascade   • 95 Foot Drop

This falls is well worth the difficult walk. Hundreds of small shelves are formed from stratified sandstone of the Thunderhead Formation. The layers of rock are horizontal. The water of Little Creek presents a big show as it falls off the side of Thomas Ridge near Deeplow Gap.

The main flow of water falls straight down the middle of the rock with a lesser stream to the left. The 25 foot wide cascade spreads to 40 feet at its base, where a log acts as both dam and bridge making a small pool and a way across the creek. Moss covered logs and rhododendron frame this picture of falling water. Doghobble and ferns are in abundance in the primarily hardwood forest.

The trail passes near the top of the falls and crosses the creek at the base. It's amazing that such a small creek can create such a large wonder.

To Get There: 13.6 or 3 mile roundtrip DIFFICULT hikes.

Both routes are steep and difficult walking. The first one begins at the Deep Creek Campground. Walk up the Deep Creek Trail past Toms Branch Falls 0.9 miles to the Indian Creek Trail. Turn right onto the Indian Creek Trail near Indian Creek Falls. Both trails are jeep roads that provide easy walking. The Indian Creek Trail follows its namesake, ascending 3.7 miles to Deeplow Gap Trail. Go to the right and cross Indian Creek via a bridge.

Ascend Thomas Ridge following Georges Branch on a graded jeep road. After 0.3 miles the trail goes to the left but the road veers right. Leave the road to go up to Deeplow Gap which is reached at 6 miles. The trail intersects the Thomas Divide Trail here. Continue east (straight ahead) to descend along Little Creek. The top of the cascade is reached at 6.5 miles and the bottom is 0.2 miles on down after a switchback.

The other route begins at the end of Cooper Creek Road. This route is shorter but you must park on private property. Ask for permission at the trout farm. The Cooper Creek Road, in the Ela community, is 5.7 miles west from the intersection of Highways 441 and 19 in Cherokee. Drive 3 miles up the Cooper Creek Road.

The trailhead is at the end of the road. This trail can be wet at times. Walk 0.5 miles up a rocky roadbed to a trail intersection. Take the left fork which climbs up Thomas Ridge 1 mile to the base of the cascade. This is a short but steep walk.

"Down, down, down! And never a sign that man had ever been here before us, except along the narrow track we followed. The torrent alongside us dashed over ledges and boulders with hiss and roar. The crossings became difficult. There was nowhere a footlog; so we had to jump from one waterworn rock to another, in our smooth-soled shoes. The submerged rocks were slippery as grease. If one of us had fallen, the others might have had to make a litter to bear him out."

-From "Raid Into Sugarlands" in
Our Southern Highlanders
by Horace Kephart, 1913.

▲ *Little Creek Falls*

Fontana

Fontana Village is a resort area that was built from the housing used by workers during the construction of Fontana Dam. On the west end of the park, follow Highway 129 from the Foothills Parkway or Maryville to Highway 28 at Deals Gap. Then turn onto Highway 28 for the 11 miles to Fontana. Beautiful overlooks abound on Highways 129 and 28 which go 24 miles from the intersection of 129 and the Foothills Parkway to Fontana Village. From Cherokee take Highway 19 through Bryson City until it intersects Highway 28 which goes to Fontana.

Visit Fontana Dam, the highest dam in the Tennessee Valley Authority system at 480 feet. The dam was built in the 1940s to supply Alcoa and Oak Ridge with power. The Appalachian Trail passes over the dam on its way into the national park. Fontana is one of the quieter spots in the Smokies, attracting many fishermen to the lake and creeks. map is on page 78.

Twentymile Cascade
•Cascade   •22 Foot Drop/95 Foot Run

Twentymile is an undisturbed, secluded spot in the park. Even though Twentymile Cascade is relatively small, it is beautiful. The cascade, which is 100 yards above the junction of Twentymile Creek and Moore Springs Branch, is a series of uneven ledges. The 20 foot wide creek spills over a series of zig-zag ledges which act as switchbacks.

Notice the small, forceful flow to the left, undercutting the rocks and trees. When the water level is high, it surrounds a large boulder before forming a 25 foot diameter pool. The creek then drops 6 feet while running through a 20 foot boulder field.

After a drop of 4 feet over a moss covered ledge, the creek slides down a perfectly formed ledge. This last ledge is 12 feet high and 25 feet wide with a 45° tilt away from the base. This tilt allows the water to spread evenly and slide to the last pool. Twentymile Creek turns slightly to the right as large boulders on the left squeeze it back to a normal size. This speeds the flow as the water rushes to meet Moore Springs Branch.

The exposed sandstone is criss-crossed with streaks of quartz. Above the main cascade (130 feet) is a small falls where the creek is only 10 feet wide. The water drops 6 feet over a rounded stone outcropping completely surrounding it with an even flow. In dry weather a stone splits the creek to form two small falls. The area is dense with rhododendron and hemlock which provide greenery all year round. See the photo on page 52.

It's said Twentymile Creek gets its name because it is twenty miles downstream from the mouth of Hazel Creek. Others have said that it was because the creek was thought to drain twenty miles through the mountains.

This easy walk is a nice stop on the way to Fontana or after taking the Parson Branch Road out of Cades Cove.

To Get There: A 1 mile roundtrip EASY walk

The Twentymile Ranger Station is on North Carolina Highway 28 three miles east of the junction of Highway 129 at Deals Gap and 6.2 miles west of Fontana Dam. This is about 18.5 miles from the west end of the Foothills Parkway at Highway 129.

Two parking areas are available, one below the Ranger Station and one above. Follow the jeep road past the Ranger Station to the gate. This is an easy walk of 0.4 miles to the junction of Wolf Ridge Trail. Continue to the right for another 100 yards to the sign marking the Twentymile Cascade, which is below the trail to the right.

The entire trail is a gravel jeep road which makes for easy walking. In spring, wildflowers abound including foam flower, trillium, fire pink, doghobble and buttercups. Return to the car by the same trail.

Hazel Creek Cascade
•Cascade •25 Foot Drop/80 Foot Run

Hazel Creek Cascade is located on the upper reaches of Hazel Creek on the side of Welch Ridge. Below an old backcountry campsite the water of Hazel Creek tumbles over sandstone ledges in a peaceful and remote area. A footlog crosses Hazel Creek at the top of the cascade. Here the creek is squeezed to the left in a small gutter. The water then runs to the right and spreads to 10 feet as it drops over a 15 foot ledge which is the first and largest. This falls is pictured on page 48.

The plunge pool at the base is quite deep and 20 feet wide. From the pool the creek narrows back to 8 feet as it rushes over large boulders and ledges dropping 6 to 8 feet over a 75 foot run. The creek then drops 8 feet over another ledge to a small pool. The water is quickly squeezed into a forceful flow in a gutter only 4 feet wide.

Take note of the layers in the sandstone on the last ledge. The strata are vertical which indicates some upheaval that forced the rock upward. After this interesting feature the water winds its way down to Fontana Lake.

To Get There: A 26 or 15 mile roundtrip DIFFICULT hike.

Begin by hiring a boat at the Fontana Boat Dock outside of Fontana Village. The boat can be hired any day from 8 A.M. to 3:30 P.M. year round. To make reservations call (704)498-2211 Ext. 277. Cross the lake to Hazel Creek trail which is a good jeep road. The walk along Hazel Creek is gentle and beautiful. Walk through historic Proctor, the site of logging operations, in the earlier part of this century. Although very little remains of this thriving community, over 1000 people lived there in the boom days.

The trail follows Hazel Creek all the way to the cascades. The grade is gentle but long. Numerous opportunities to enjoy the creek are available all along this very popular fishing stream. Anglers frequent the rushing waters for good catches. The remoteness of the area lends itself to an abundance of wildlife.

Evidences of the old logging days can be seen along the trail all the way to the cascades. Twisted rails and an old railroad bed are at the foot of the cascades. Five backcountry campsites are on the trail. Some of these are open to horses, others to foot travelers only. Spend a few days in this once populated, now remote region.

Another route to the cascades begins at the Forney Ridge Parking Area at Clingmans Dome. This second route is a strenuous walk along the Appalachian Trail but affords many scenic vistas into North Carolina and Tennessee. From the parking area walk up to the Appalachian Trail at Clingmans Dome. Follow the AT 4.2 miles to the Welch Ridge Trail (this is east of Silers Bald). When last at this junction, the sign was on the ground.

Take the Welch Ridge Trail 1.3 miles to its junction with the upper end of the Hazel Creek Trail which goes off to the right. Walk 1.5 miles down the Hazel Creek Trail to the cascade which is reached at a footlog. This part of the walk drops nearly 1,000 feet in elevation. Remember the return trip will climb 2,600 feet back to Clingmans Dome over 7 miles of trail.

Although the cascade is small, it is a beautiful and secluded spot. Few have discovered this gem.

Artificial Waterfalls

The earliest settlers saw the potential use of the falling waters of the Smokies. Crude mills to grind grain into meal were among the first buildings erected after houses and barns. In the most remote areas farmers built their own small mills alongside mountain creeks.

The idea behind a mill was to take advantage of the natural fall of water to push a wheel. Usually the fall was enhanced by building a sluice or mill race to carry the water at a lesser slope than the creek. When a good "head" was built, the water was directed downward to strike a wheel and power a mill.

Three types of mills are found in the park. The tub mill was popular in the area. This small mill was often constructed by one family for use by a few households. LeConte Creek (once known as Mill Creek) boasted thirteen tub mills. It's said that one reason so many mills were built in such a short distance was that no one trusted his neighbor (or kin) to be fair with the toll, which was usually one gallon per bushel or 1/8th.

The tub mills had a horizontal wheel and a vertical shaft. Water struck the wheel which was usually enclosed in a wooden "tub." However, many explanations as to the derivation of the name have been offered. One is that the wheel is a turbine, thus tub is a shortened form. Another concerns how much one of these small grist mills could turn out in a day - a tub full. Yet another speaks of the wooden enclosure around the two grindstones.

▲ *Cable Mill*

Whatever the explanation, these small grist mills dotted the mountains, allowing farmers to use falling water to produce meal from grain. The Reagan and Noah "Bud" Ogle mills near Gatlinburg are two present day examples.

A second type of grist mill is the turbine mill. Although similar to the tub mill, it was more efficient because the water was confined to the turbine within a metal casing. The machinery was not homemade, but manufactured. Mingus Mill, near Cherokee, North Carolina, is a surviving turbine mill.

The overshot wheel is most commonly thought of when grist mills are mentioned. A sluice or flume directs water over the top of a vertical wheel which has wooden compartments called buckets. A horizontal shaft turns gears and the mill stones inside the building. This was a more efficient use of gravity and water to produce power. Cable Mill in Cades Cove is the only overshot mill within the park. It not only ground grain but powered a sawmill as well.

Another type of artificial waterfall is the dam. Sometimes streams would be dammed to power grist mills. Other places were dammed to move downed timber toward sawmills. The water from a river or creek was held back, then released to wash the felled trees downstream. Dams have also been built to generate electricity. Two interesting examples of these are on the borders of the park at Fontana and Waterville. It's no surprise that when the park was formed cartographers had to rename numerous Mill Creeks. Only two remain, one in Tennessee and one in North Carolina. Today the few remaining mills stand as symbols of the ingenuity of people in using the water and fall of the land to work for them.

Cable Mill

The John P. Cable Mill is located in Cades Cove half way around the one-way loop at the Cades Cove Visitor Center. Its 10 foot overshot waterwheel provided power for a sawmill as well as a grain mill. The 16 by 24 foot building is the original structure on the original site. Some restoration has been conducted to keep the mill in working order. Grain is still ground at the mill which was constructed in 1868 about one year after John P. Cable moved to Cades Cove. His son, James V. Cable, inherited the mill upon his father's death. A canal was dug from Forge Creek to Mill Creek to provide plenty of water to the mill in dry months.

Water falls 12 feet to push the 10 foot wooden wheel which pushes the inner workings of the mill. Notice the mill stones beside the walkway from the visitor center to the mill.

Noah "Bud" Ogle Mill

Noah "Bud" and Cindy Ogle, descendants of the first settlers of the area, started farming 400 acres in 1879. The preserved remains of their farm are located 2.7 miles up Airport Road from light #8 in Gatlinburg. The tub mill is located about 0.25 miles from the parking area on LeConte Creek (once called Mill Creek due to the many mills along its banks). An interpretive brochure guides you over the Ogle's farm which locals called "Junglebrook" due to the dense growth of rosebay rhododendron.

A small 10 x 10 foot, two-leveled log building houses the tub mill. A 125 foot flume crafted of hollowed logs runs from a log which dams the stream down to the penstock. The water is then directed to the 30 inch wooden, iron-rimmed wheel. The water falls 8 feet providing the power to turn the horizontal waterwheel. This reconstruction is based on photographs of the original mill.

Reagan Mill

Reagan Mill is located on the Roaring Fork Auto Tour near Gatlinburg. Turn at light #8 to go up Airport Road into the park. Pass the Noah "Bud" Ogle place (see above) to the Cherokee Orchard Road. The gate to the one-way Roaring Fork Auto Tour is 3.7 miles from the light in Gatlinburg. A booklet which describes the sights and history of the area is available in a box at the gate for a small fee. The auto tour road is closed in the winter.

Alfred Reagan's mill is beside the road on Roaring Fork Creek 3 miles from the gate. Built after the turn of the century, this small 12 by 15 foot building was one of Reagan's many enterprises. He ran a farm, a blacksmith shop and a store. The flume carries water 74 feet before dropping it 10 feet onto the 32 inch wooden tub wheel. Look under the mill to see the horizontal wheel which pushed the mill stone. The mill and the house on the opposite side of the road were constructed of lumber sawed at a water-powered sawmill in Gatlinburg near the mouth of Roaring Fork.

Alfred Reagan married Martha Bales and had seven children. Martha Bales Reagan was the granddaughter of Daniel Wesley Reagan (1802 - 1892) who was the first child born in what is now Gatlinburg. Martha's brothers, Jim and Ephraim, lived on two farms up the creek. The Alfred Reagan mill displays how one family diversified their interests to survive in the mountains.

Mingus Mill

Mingus Mill is north of the Oconaluftee Visitor Center off the Newfound Gap Road. The first mill on the sight was built in the 1790s when the Mingus family settled the area. This original mill was powered by Mingus Creek pouring onto an overshot waterwheel. The present mill was constructed in 1886 by Sion T. Early, a millwright hired by Dr. John Mingus. Early's initials can be seen on the front gable of the three story building.

The water is channeled from Mingus Creek along a wood-lined canal. It then flows into a flume which carries it 200 feet to the mill. The water falls 25 feet to shoot onto the turbine. Walk under the building to get a good look at this unusual type of mill. A brochure is available to give more details about the history and operation of this historic mill.

Mingus Mill ▲

A park volunteer or seasonal worker runs the mill from 9 to 5 daily from mid-March to mid-November. The pot-bellied stove warms the first floor on cool days while corn is ground. Due to government regulations the meal which is produced can't be sold. However, stone ground wheat and corn meal which are produced elsewhere are available for a modest price.

Fontana Dam

Fontana Dam, on the Little Tennessee River, is the highest dam east of the Mississippi River at 480 feet. It was constructed by the Tennessee Valley Authority in cooperation with the Aluminum Company of America in 1942 - 1945 to generate electricity for the production of aluminum. The waters impounded by the dam forced the removal of over 600 families.

The name Fontana means "fountain" in Italian and Late Latin. It's said that it was named for the many waterfalls in the area that look like fountains as the water leaps from rock to rock. Another story is that it was named for Felice Fontana, an Italian naturalist of the 1700s.

TVA now operates the dam to generate electricity, to provide a recreational lake and to control flooding. Visitors can tour the powerhouse and a shop at the top of the dam. The Appalachian Trail crosses the dam on the 2,100 mile trek from Georgia to Maine. The dam is an amazing sight from a vantage point high atop the concrete structure.

Walters Dam and Powerhouse

Walters Dam and Power Plant is the largest power plant operated by the Carolina Power and Light Company. The powerhouse, which is located beside Interstate 40 near the North Carolina - Tennessee State Line, is 12 miles downstream from the dam. The dam directs the water of the Pigeon River down a 14 foot diameter tunnel 6.7 miles through the solid rock of the mountains. The total drop in elevation from the dam to the powerhouse is 800 feet. The last 600 feet is a sheer drop from the top of the mountain to the generators. When completed in 1930, after three years of construction, Walters Dam and Powerhouse had the highest fall of water to a generator east of the Mississippi River. The power plant can generate 105,000 megawatts.

Take the Waterville exit to get a closer look at this powerhouse that sits beside a river that appears to come from nowhere.

Auto Viewing of Waterfalls and Cascades

Many opportunities for viewing waterfalls and cascades from the window of your car exist in the park. Several drives in the park highlight creeks and rivers. Below are suggestions of some of the best drives:

Little River Road (Highway 73) - The trip from Townsend to Gatlinburg is a beautiful one. The highway follows the Little River for 12 miles. The Sinks and Meigs Falls are passed on this route which has many small falls and cascades. Kayaks and canoes share the river with swimmers and sunbathers. Metcalf Bottoms Picnic Area provides a wonderful place to enjoy the river and a meal.

Elkmont - The entrance to Elkmont is 5 miles from the Sugarlands Visitor Center on the Little River Road (Highway 73). The road follows the Little River into the Elkmont vacation community. Huskey Branch Cascade is in this area. See page 34 for details.

Tremont - Drive the five miles up the Middle Prong of the Little River to where Lynn Camp Prong and Thunderhead Prong join. Begin 0.2 miles from the intersection of the Little River Road (Highway 73) with the Laurel Creek Road. Drive past the Tremont Ranger Station and the Great Smoky Mountains Institute to the site of a logging community. This drive is a self guided auto tour. The river is beautiful. Trails to Indian Flats, Spruce Flats and Lynn Camp Prong Falls are on this road. See pages 38-43.

Laurel Creek Road - This 7 mile road goes from Townsend to Cades Cove. Part of it follows the picturesque Laurel Creek. The road twists and turns alongside the creek.

Parson Branch Road - An eight mile gravel road which is a one-way exit from Cades Cove. Turn off the Cades Cove Loop Road near the Cades Cove Visitor Center. Turn to the right and go over a bridge to begin this road which literally splashes across Panther Creek and Parson Branch a number of times. This is a wonderful drive when the rhododendrons are in bloom. The road ends on Highway 129 near Calderwood and Chilhowee Lakes. Enjoy views of the lakes on a return trip along Highway 129 and the Foothills Parkway. Twentymile Creek and Fontana are to the left on Highway 129. This road is closed during the winter months.

Newfound Gap Road (Highway 441) - This major thoroughfare between Gatlinburg and Cherokee is often crowded. Stop often to enjoy the creeks and rivers on this route. From Gatlinburg the West Prong of the Little Pigeon River is followed to the Alum Cave Trail Parking area. After that Walker Camp Prong is beside the road. The first pull-off on the North Carolina side of Newfound Gap sits across the headwaters of the Oconaluftee River. Descend Thomas Ridge to follow the Oconaluftee to Cherokee.

Roaring Fork Motor Nature Trail - For a small fee, purchase a booklet which describes the natural and human history of the area. The 5.5 mile road is winding and narrow but paved and well cared for. It provides access to Baskins Creek and Grotto Falls along with beautiful stretches of Roaring Fork. The Place of a Thousand Drips can be seen from the car. The auto trail is located off Cherokee Orchard Road near Gatlinburg. Turn at Light #8 to go up Airport Road and Cherokee Orchard.

Greenbrier - The Greenbrier area can be reached off Highway 321 six miles from Gatlinburg. The road follows the Little Pigeon River past the ranger station to a junction which is 3.2 miles from the highway. The road becomes a gravel road after the ranger station. Turn left at the bridge to ride 1.5 miles beside the Middle Prong of the Little Pigeon River to reach the beginning of the Ramsay Cascade Trail. This secluded area is popular for picnics. Fern Branch Falls is up the Porters Creek Trail.

Mileage Chart

Gatlinburg	Cherokee	Townsend	Cosby (campground)	Maryville	Cades Cove	Fontana	Pigeon Forge
34							
22	54						
20	54	42					
41	74	20	60				
25	56	9	45	29			
64	44	42	84	64	51		
8	42	15	28	35	24	57	

Resources

Most of the following resources are available at the visitor centers in the Great Smoky Mountains National Park.

National Park Literature and Brochures (Most cost 25¢ to 50¢) One is entitled "Streams and Waterfalls."

Smokies Guide The official newspaper of Great Smoky Mountains National Park.

Great Smoky Mountains Handbook 112 One of the best introductions to the park. It's a National Park Handbook.

Mountain Roads and Quiet Places by Jerry DeLaughter. A complete guide to the roads of the Great Smoky Mountains National Park. This is the official guide to the roads but it contains much more.

A Roadside Guide to the Geology of the Great Smoky Mountains National Park by Harry L. Moore. A great introduction to the geology of the park with five road tours and five hikes.

Time Well Spent Family Hiking In The Smokies by Hal Hubbs, Charles Maynard and David Morris. A good introductory trail guide to 25 hikes for adults and children.

Hiking in the Great Smokies by Carson Brewer. One of the better guides available.

A Wonderment of Mountains: The Great Smokies by Carson Brewer. A collection of columns about hiking, history, flora and fauna.

Great Smoky Mountains Wildflowers by Carlos Campbell, William F. Hutson, & Aaron J. Sharp. U.T. Press. An easy to carry pictorial guide to many common wildflowers.

Strangers in High Places by Michael Frome. A good history of the Great Smoky Mountains.

Our Southern Highlanders by Horace Kephart. A classic written in the early 1900s by one who worked to establish the park.

The Cades Cove Story by Randolph Shields. A short history of the white settlement in Cades Cove.

Exploring the Smokies by Rose Houk. Things to see and do in the Great Smoky Mountains.

Trails Illustrated Topo Map of the Great Smoky Mountains National Park. A plastic map which is one of the most up to date maps there is.

Great Smoky Mountains National Park Recreation Map by Trails Illustrated. A good paper map for day use which is coordinated with this book and Time Well Spent.

Hiking Trails of the Smokies by the Great Smoky Mountains Natural History Association. The only comprehensive guide to the trails of the park. The best guide available.

Cades Cove/Townsend
Spruce Flats Falls • Lynn Camp Prong Cascades
•Indian Flats Falls • Abrams Falls

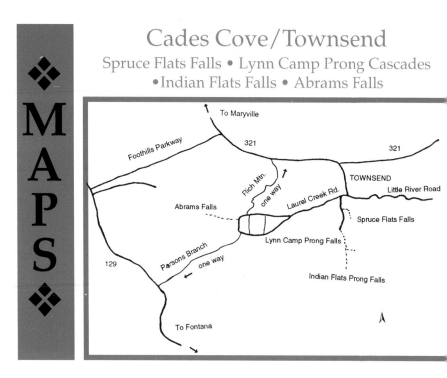

Gatlinburg
Ramsay Cascade • Fern Branch Falls • Rainbow Falls
• Baskins Creek Falls • Grotto Falls • Place Of A Thousand
Drips • Cataract Falls • The Sinks • Laurel Falls • Huskey
Branch Cascade • Meigs Falls

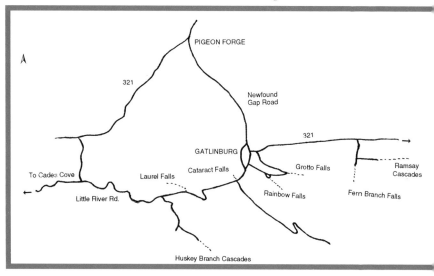

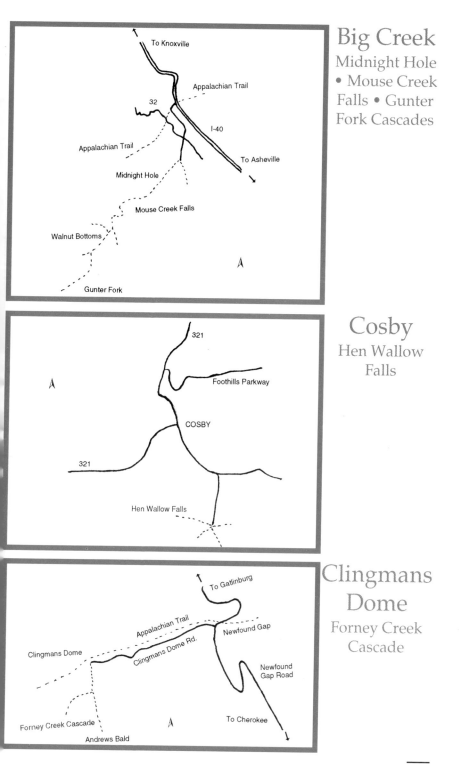

Big Creek
Midnight Hole • Mouse Creek Falls • Gunter Fork Cascades

To Knoxville

Appalachian Trail

32

I-40

Appalachian Trail

To Asheville

Midnight Hole

Mouse Creek Falls

Walnut Bottoms

Gunter Fork

Cosby
Hen Wallow Falls

321

Foothills Parkway

COSBY

321

Hen Wallow Falls

Clingmans Dome
Forney Creek Cascade

To Gatlinburg

Appalachian Trail

Newfound Gap

Clingmans Dome

Clingmans Dome Rd.

Newfound Gap Road

Forney Creek Cascade

Andrews Bald

To Cherokee

Cherokee - Deep Creek

Chasteen Creek • Mingo Falls • Flat Creek Falls
• Juneywhank Falls • Toms Branch Falls • Indian Creek Falls
• Little Creek Falls

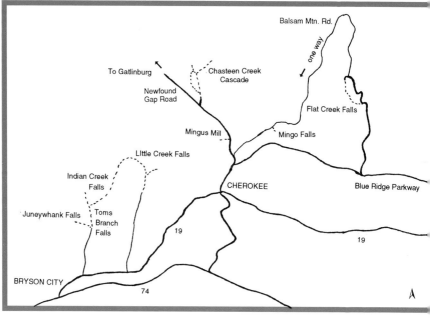

Fontana

Twentymile Creek Cascade • Hazel Creek Cascade

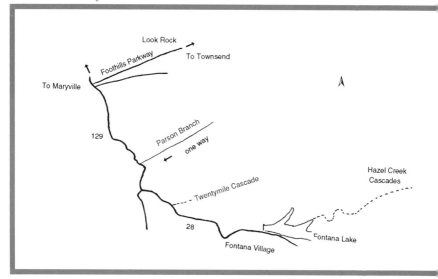

By the Same Authors...

Time Well Spent
Family Hiking in the Smokies

"Family hiking doesn't have to be a frustrating struggle, but it does involve more than just walking a mountain trail. The key to enjoyment is planning ahead." Time Well Spent assists families in planning for walks in the Smokies with 25 enjoyable hikes for all types of families, 7 maps with good directions to all areas of the national park, 15 short nature and historical trails which reveal life in the Smokies then and now, suggestions for finding waterfalls, firetowers, historic buildings, wildflowers, virgin forest and scenic views. Included are interesting stories and legends about the region and a handy index for quick reference.

This is what others are saying about Time Well Spent....

❖ *"This book is certainly necessary if you plan on taking your family hiking in the Smokies...It would be money well spent on Time Well Spent."*
    - David Carroll WBIR Channel 3 Chattanooga, TN.

❖ *"Here's a brief but handy guide to 25 hikes a family can trek together plus details on short nature and historical trails."*
    - S. Keith Graham Atlanta Journal/Constitution

❖ *"Another stocking stuffer for all ages is Time Well Spent - Family Hiking in the Smokies...Great gift for any outdoorsman on your list!"*
    - Sue McClure Nashville Banner

❖ *"Time Well Spent - Family Hiking in the Smokies is a user-friendly paperback written in a breezy, engaging style...Even if you never plan to hike these mountain trails, just reading the book is time well spent."*
    - Ruth Robinson The Chattanooga Times

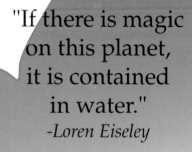

"If there is magic
on this planet,
it is contained
in water."
-Loren Eiseley